:30 MINUTE NECKLACES

 **MINUTE NECKLACES**

▶ **60 Quick & Creative Projects for Jewelers**

Marthe Le Van

LARK
CRAFTS

A Division of Sterling Publishing Co., Inc.
New York / London

Assistant Editor
Gavin R. Young

Technical Editor
Joanna Gollberg

Art Director
Kristi Pfeffer

Designer
Ginger Graziano

Photographer
Stewart O'Shields

Cover Designer
Ginger Graziano

Library of Congress Cataloging-in-Publication Data

Le Van, Marthe.
　30-minute necklaces : 60 quick & creative projects for jewelers / Marthe Le Van. -- 1st ed.
　　p. cm.
　Includes index.
　ISBN 978-1-60059-489-2 (pb-trade pbk. : alk. paper)
　1. Jewelry making. 2. Necklaces. I. Title. II. Title: Thirty-minute necklaces.
　TT212.L4884 2010
　739.27--dc22

　　　　　　　　　　2009052367

10 9 8 7 6 5 4 3 2 1

First Edition

Published by Lark Books, A Division of
Sterling Publishing Co., Inc.
387 Park Avenue South, New York, NY 10016

Text, photography, and illustrations © 2010, Lark Books, a Division of Sterling Publishing Co., Inc.

Distributed in Canada by Sterling Publishing,
c/o Canadian Manda Group, 165 Dufferin Street
Toronto, Ontario, Canada M6K 3H6

Distributed in the United Kingdom by GMC Distribution Services,
Castle Place, 166 High Street, Lewes, East Sussex, England BN7 1XU

Distributed in Australia by Capricorn Link (Australia) Pty Ltd.,
P.O. Box 704, Windsor, NSW 2756 Australia

If you have questions or comments about this book, please contact:
Lark Books
67 Broadway
Asheville, NC 28801
828-253-0467

Manufactured in China

ISBN 13: 978-1-60059-489-2

For information about custom editions, special sales, and premium and corporate purchases, please contact the Sterling Special Sales Department at 800-805-5489 or specialsales@sterlingpub.com.

For information about desk and examination copies available to college and university professors, requests must be submitted to academic@larkbooks.com. Our complete policy can be found at www.larkbooks.com.

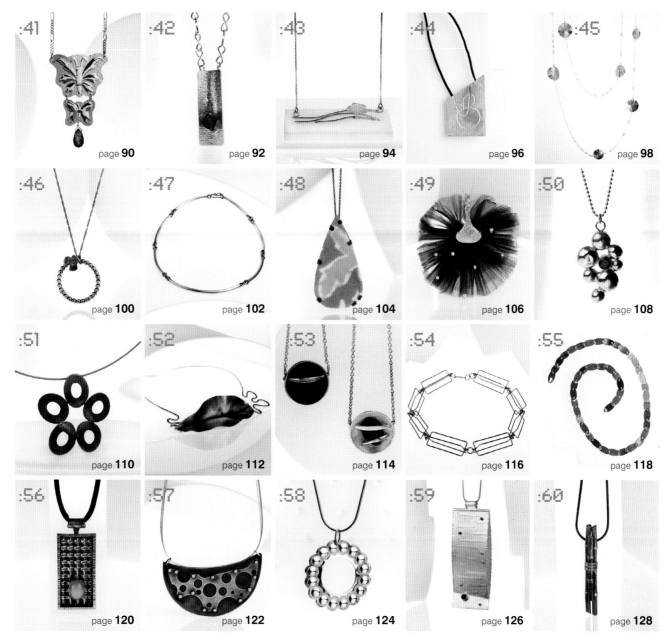

Introduction

Time is a precious commodity that seems to always have the winning hand. Not in this case! A ticking clock should never stand in the way of looking great, so we've developed a series of jewelry books that offers tons of projects to make in 30 minutes or less. First in the series was *30-Minute Earrings* (Lark, 2010), and now we're thrilled to introduce an equally fabulous collection of projects in *30-Minute Necklaces*. This book gives you reason to escape from the crazy world for half an hour to create a necklace or pendant that will please you or a lucky recipient for years to come. The half second it takes to secure the clasp on your new creation will always remind you of how easy it is to look good.

One of the most compelling things about *30-Minute Necklaces* is that it's full of surprises. First, the variety of styles that can be achieved with these projects is remarkable. Some are delicate and sophisticated, such as the sterling silver linked chain by Monika Becker (page 77), and others are bold and cutting edge, such as Sun Young Cheong's blue tutu necklace dotted with pearls (page 106). With necklaces and pendants generally being large statement pieces (as compared to their smaller earring and bracelet counterparts), you'd think they'd take hours to craft, but the ingenuity in these projects makes that not the case. Many of them come with easy-to-copy templates that serve as simple springboards to the designs.

Another component that will catch your attention is the diversity of designers willing to share their one-of-a-kind ideas. Asheville, North Carolina–based designer Joanna Gollberg is the author of four Lark books, including *The Ultimate Jeweler's Guide* (2010), which is a great resource for anyone interested in brushing up on basic metalworking techniques, materials, and tools. Peter Hoogeboom, a designer from Amsterdam, has shown his work in museums and galleries around the globe, and his slate disk pendants (page 65) are a testament to his expertise. Finally, if you're a fan of chain mail, you'll recognize award-winning designer and instructor Rebeca Mojica's work (page 23). We're also pleased to include up-and-coming talents like Sara Westermark, a self-taught jeweler whose two featured necklaces are absolutely striking (pages 112 and 122).

The next pleasant surprise you'll encounter in *30-Minute Necklaces* involves our friend, cash money. Many of the supplies and tools used are quite affordable, and you very likely have some of them on hand, particularly if you're already a jewelry hobbyist. One pendant is actually made from a scrap of wallpaper, while another uses craft foam as the primary material. As for the tools, we list items that would be found in your basic

bench tool kit and soldering kit, but you definitely don't need every single item to make these pieces. You may even choose to make particular projects because you already have the materials and tools—not a bad idea! If you do invest money in materials, you can always plan to have enough left to make a variation. Several projects are accompanied by an image of a similar design.

Now, a quick note on the book's organization. Since it's all about saving time, we're not getting into the basics of jewelry making; we assume you either already know the tricks of the trade, or you'll find out! Instead, you jump right into the projects. With each design, you'll find a **Get Ready** heading followed by the short list of skills required to complete the project. Under **Get Set**, you'll see the necessary tools and materials needed to make it. Step by step instructions are under the **Go** heading.

And now it's time to do just that. Grab your tools, set your stopwatch, and Go!

Bench Tool Kit

Bench pin

Steel bench block

Jeweler's saw frame

Saw blades

Beeswax

Needle files

Bastard file

Sandpaper, 220 and 400 grit

Emery paper

Chasing hammer

Rawhide or wooden mallet

Forging hammer

Mandrels

Dapping block and punches

Flexible shaft

Wood block

Drill bits

Burrs

Scribe

Stainless steel ruler

Dividers

Calipers

Pliers

Wire cutters

Center punch

Burnisher

Safety glasses

Safety gloves

Hearing protection

Dust mask

Soldering Kit

Soldering torch

Striker

Heat resistant soldering surfaces (charcoal blocks, firebricks, or ceramic plates)

Flux

Flux brush or other applicator

Solder (hard, medium, and easy)

Snips

Small embroidery scissors

Solder pick

Tweezers

Cross-locking tweezers with wooden handle

Third hand

Copper tongs

Water for quenching

Pickle

Pickle warming pot

Safety glasses

Fire extinguisher

➤➤ **Get Set**

Gold-plated slant tube
bead, 6 x 18 mm

Sterling silver rolo chain,
2.5 mm, 20 inches
(51 cm)

Sterling silver jump ring,
18 gauge, 5 mm

Faceted metallic bicone
crystal bead, 4 mm

7 sterling silver headpins,
24 gauge, each 1 inch
(2.5 cm)

6 faceted metallic bicone
crystal beads, each
3 mm

2 sterling silver split rings,
each 7 mm

Sterling silver lobster clasp,
5 x 9 mm

Bench tool kit, page 9

FINISHED SIZE
Lariat necklace,
17 inches (43.2 cm)

➤➤➤ **Go**

1. Measure and use a center punch and hammer to mark a point on the inside of the tube bead that is approximately 2 mm below the rim at the top of the bead. Drill a hole at the marked point.

2. Use snips to cut a 20-inch (50.8 cm) length of rolo chain. Connect one end of the chain to the drilled hole in the tube bead with the 5-mm jump ring. Slide the other end of the chain through the tube.

3. Thread the 4-mm bicone crystal bead onto a headpin. Use a basic wrapped loop to attach the headpin to the last link of the rolo chain. This link will be link number 1.

4. Thread the six 3-mm bicone crystal beads onto six headpins. Use a basic wrapped loop to attach one bead each to link numbers 3, 5, 11, 15, 27, and 45.

5. Use snips to cut the chain 8 inches (20.3 cm) from the 5-mm jump ring. Use needle-nose pliers to attach a split ring to each of the chain ends and the lobster clasp to one of the split rings.

SAWING • FILING • SANDING • DAPPING
PLANISHING • DRILLING • BURNISHING

▶▶ ▶ Get Set

Fine silver sheet, 12 gauge,
1¼ x 1½ inches
(3.2 x 3.8 cm)

Fine silver sheet,
12 gauge, ½ x ¾ inch
(1.3 x 1.9 cm)

Sterling silver snake chain
with clasp, 1.2 mm,
18 inches (45.7 cm)

Bench tool kit, page 9

Wooden dapping block

Pear shaped, plastic-head
mallet

Planishing hammer

Dapping punches,
approximately 21.4 and
19.8 mm

Steel dapping punches,
approximately 11.9,
10.3, and 8.7 mm

FINISHED SIZE
Pendant, 1½ x 1¼ inches
(3.8 x 3.2 cm)

▶ ▶ ▶ Go

1. Use a scribe or a permanent marker to draw an oval on each piece of silver sheet, using as much space on the sheet as possible. Cut out each oval with a jeweler's saw. File and sand the cut edges.

2. Using the pear shaped plastic mallet and the wood dapping block, sink the two silver ovals until they begin to take on a cup form.

3. Place the larger oval over a steel dapping punch that is approximately 24.6 mm. Using a planishing hammer, raise the cup form, starting from the bottom and moving towards the lip. Planish lightly to keep the metal as thick as possible, and take care to keep the oval shape.

4. Switch to a smaller dapping punch, approximately 21.4 mm, and repeat step 3. Finish raising the cup with a third, smaller dapping punch, approximately 19.8 mm. Keep the textured, planished surface on the metal. When fully raised, the large cup should be ¾ inch (1.9 cm) tall.

5. Raise a second cup from the smaller silver oval using a series of steel dapping punches that are approximately 11.9 mm, 10.3 mm, and 8.7 mm. The small cup should be ¼ inch (6 mm) tall.

6. On the closed, domed end of the large silver cup, measure and mark a ½ x ¾-inch (1.3 x 1.9 cm) oval. Measure and mark a 1½ x 1¼-inch (3.8 x 3.2 cm) oval on the closed, domed end of the small silver cup.

7. Drill a small hole inside each marked oval with a 0.5-mm bit. Cut out each marked oval with a jeweler's saw. File and sand a beveled edge on each silver piece.

8. Burnish the beveled cup edges, and thread both silver forms onto the snake chain.

►► **Get Set**

Antique brass oval jump ring or link from chain, 5 x 10 mm

Antique brass cable chain, 3 x 2 mm, 4½ inches (11.4 cm)

2 antique brass jump rings, 10 gauge, each 8 mm

6 copper jump rings, 20 gauge, each 5 mm

Black rubber O-ring, 14 gauge, 20 mm

3 black anodized aluminum jump rings, 18 gauge, each 7 mm

Silver-gold aluminum scale stamping, 20 gauge, 1 x ¾ inch (2.5 x 1.9 cm)

Black rubber O-ring, 14 gauge, 20 mm

2 black anodized aluminum jump rings, 20 gauge, each 4 mm

6 antique brass jump rings, 18 gauge, each 6 mm

Silver-gold aluminum scale, ⁷⁄₁₆ x ½ inch (1.1 x 1.3 cm)

Bronze aluminum scale, ⁷⁄₁₆ x ½ inch (1.1 x 1.3 cm)

Antique copper curb chain, 5 mm, 4½ inches (11.4 cm)

Antique brass cable chain, 10 x 5 mm, 9 inches (22.9 cm)

Natural brass rolo chain, 3 mm, 4½ inches (11.4 cm)

19 antique brass jump rings, 20 gauge, 4 mm

5 black rubber O-rings, 14 gauge, each 12 mm

4 copper jump rings, 20 gauge, each 6 mm

Antique brass lobster clasp, 8 mm

2 pairs of chain-nose pliers

Snips

FINISHED SIZE
Pendant, 2¼ x 1 inch
(5.7 x 2.5 cm)

►►► **Go**

Making the Pendant

1. Use the chain-nose pliers to attach one 5 x 10-mm oval link from the brass chain to two brass 8-mm jump rings. Attach three 5-mm copper jump rings to the 8-mm brass rings and one 12-mm O-ring to the 5-mm copper rings.

2. Use the chain-nose pliers to attach one black 7-mm jump ring to the bottom of the 12-mm O-ring. Attach the silver-gold stamping (horizontally), the 20-mm O-ring, and two black 4-mm jump rings to the 7-mm black jump ring. Attach three brass 6-mm jump rings around the 20-mm O-ring and the stamping on both the right and left sides of the black 7-mm jump ring.

3. Use the chain-nose pliers to attach three 5-mm copper jump rings to the two 4-mm black jump rings. Add the silvery-gold scale and one black 7-mm jump ring to the three 5-mm copper jump rings. Make sure to attach the black jump ring so it lies on top of the scale.

4. Use the chain-nose pliers to attach one 7-mm black jump ring and the bronze scale to the bottom of the stamping and the 20-mm O-ring.

Making the Chain

5. Use snips to cut 4½-inch (11.4 cm) pieces of the copper chain, the 3-mm brass cable chain, and the brass rolo chain. String the pendant onto all three chains through the 5 x 10-mm oval brass link.

6. Attach one 4-mm brass jump ring to each end of each chain and also to one 12-mm O-ring. Attach these elements to the 12-mm black O-ring in the following order: two 4-mm brass jump rings, two 6-mm copper jump rings, two 4-mm brass jump rings, one 12-mm O-ring, two 4-mm brass jump rings, and 4½ inches (11.4 cm) of the 5 x 10-mm cable chain.

7. Repeat step 6 with the other side of the chain, then attach one 4-mm brass jump ring and the clasp to the last link of chain.

→ Get Ready

CUTTING • GLUING • HAMMERING • WIREWORK

► Get Set

Rubber lacing, matte finish,
   3.5 mm, 58 inches
   (147.3 cm)

Super-strong gap-filling
   adhesive

Acetone

46 sterling silver round
   tube spacers, each
   6 x 3.8 mm

Sterling silver wire,
   16 gauge, 3 inches
   (7.6 cm)

Bench tool kit, page 9

FINISHED SIZE
16¼ x ⅞ inch
(41.3 x 2.2 cm)

► ► ► Go

1. Cut the rubber lacing into 46 segments, each 1¼ inches (3.2 cm) long, making sure the ends are flat. Two segments will form one ring, for a total of 23 rings.

2. Place a small drop of glue on one end of two sections of rubber. Slide the glued ends into a silver tube spacer, making sure they meet equally in the middle of the spacer. Firmly press together for 10 seconds.

3. Place a small drop of glue on the opposite ends of the two rubber segments. Bend one end into a C shape, slide the rubber to the middle of a tubing spacer, and insert the remaining rubber end into the spacer so the two ends meet. Press firmly together for 10 seconds.

4. Repeat steps 2 and 3 with the remaining rubber segments, making sure to link the subsequent rings to one another before closing the rings.

5. Use acetone to remove any excess glue from the rubber rings.

6. Hammer the ends of the 16-gauge sterling silver wire so they slightly fan out and flatten. File the ends smooth.

7. Use round-nose pliers to form a 7-mm loop at one end of the wire. Shape the remaining wire into a hook using your fingers and round-nose pliers. Use chain-nose and flat-nose pliers to open the 7-mm loop like a jump ring, and connect the clasp to the last rubber ring.

DESIGNER: **ADA ROSMAN**

▶▶ **Get Set**

Plastic bags

White photocopy or printer paper

Sewing thread, various colors

Sterling silver jump rings, 22 gauge, each 3.2 mm

Sterling silver cable chain with 2-mm clasp, 18 inches (45.7 cm)

Scissors

Iron

Ironing board

Sewing machine

Sewing pin or needle

Flat-nose pliers

Chain-nose pliers

FINISHED SIZE
From 1¾ x 1¾ inches (4.4 x 4.4 cm) to 3½ x 1½ inches (8.9 x 3.8 cm), depending on the design

▶▶▶ **Go**

1. Use scissors to cut off the handles and bottom of each plastic bag so the flat portion of each bag remains. Turn any bags with print inside out. Fold each bag three times to make the plastic eight-ply thick.

2. Place a folded bag between two sheets of white printer paper, making sure the paper covers all of the plastic. In a well-ventilated area, iron the paper and the bags on the rayon (low) setting for 10 to 15 seconds. Flip the paper and repeat. Check to ensure all layers of plastic have adhered to one another. Iron out any bubbles. Repeat this step for all of the bags.

3. Use a sewing machine to stitch random lines on the plastic sheets. Vary the thread colors as you like.

4. Use scissors to cut out circles or other shapes of varying dimensions from the sewn plastic sheets.

5. Layer the circles or lay them in a line. Use a pin to poke holes in the circles where you want to add jump rings. Use pliers to attach the jump rings to the bags. Thread the silver chain through a jump ring.

VARIATION

▶▶ **Get Set**

Soft polymer clay,
20 grams

Stainless steel tiger tail
wire, 17 inches
(43.2 cm)

Stainless steel crimp beads

Magnetic clasp

Stainless steel sewing
machine bobbin

Craft knife

Baking tray

Conventional oven or
toaster oven

Needle-nose pliers

Crimping pliers

Snips

FINISHED SIZE
Necklace, 17 inches
(43.2 cm); pendant,
¾ inch (2 cm) in diameter

▶▶▶ **Go**

1. Measure the space between the two walls of the sewing machine bobbin. Roll a 20-gram piece of polymer clay into a smooth sausage to match the measured width.

2. Bend the polymer clay sausage around the bobbin and between the two walls until the two ends meet. Press the clay down firmly to ensure it reaches the center of the bobbin. The clay should appear in the holes in the bobbin walls with no gaps, and it should reach the top of the walls.

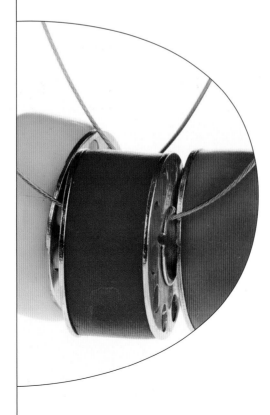

3. Cut off any excess polymer clay with a craft knife. Roll the bobbin between your fingers until the joint is invisible and the clay fills the groove evenly.

4. Following the manufacturer's instructions for the polymer clay brand you are using, bake the bobbin on a baking tray in a conventional or toaster oven. Allow the bobbin to cool, and thread the stainless steel wire through its center hole.

5. Thread one of the crimp beads followed by one half of the magnetic clasp onto one end of the wire. Loop the end of the wire back through the crimp bead and secure the bead with crimping pliers.

6. Check the necklace length, and then repeat step 5 on the other end of the wire. Use snips to trim off any excess wire near the clasp.

→ → **Get Set**

111 red anodized
aluminum jump rings,
12 gauge, each ⁷⁄₁₆ inch
(1.1 cm) ID

6 aluminum jump rings,
16 gauge, each ¼ inch
(0.6 cm) ID

5 red anodized aluminum
jump rings, 16 gauge,
each ⁵⁄₁₆ inch (8 mm) ID

Lobster claw clasp, 22 mm

2 pair flat-nose pliers,
duckbill type

FINISHED SIZE
Chain, 1 x 21 inches
(2.5 x 54 cm)

DESIGNER'S NOTES
Cover the jaws of your
pliers in masking tape to
protect the jump ring finish.

To work faster, do not
pre-open and pre-close
your rings. Instead, open
and close "raw" rings as
you go. This saves the
time of picking up a ring,
manipulating it, and putting
it back down, only to pick
it up later again. In this
"speedweaving" method,
you only touch each
ring once.

→ → → **Go**

1. Open a large red jump ring. While holding
it in the pliers, use the end of the jump ring
to scoop up two more large red rings. Close
the open jump ring and the two rings you
scooped up. This is the first unit of the weave.

2. Open a new large red jump ring, and
scoop up two large red rings. Weave this
new ring through the center ring of the first
unit and close the ring. Close the two red
rings that you scooped. Repeat this step until
all the large red jump rings are used.

3. Position one of the small, aluminum jump
rings at the very end of the chain. Connect
this jump ring to the center ring of the last
unit. Add another aluminum jump ring and
the clasp to the first aluminum jump ring.
Close each jump ring.

4. Make a simple chain using 11 small
aluminum jump rings. Connect the simple
chain to the center large red jump ring on the
opposite end of the necklace.

5. Connect one small, red aluminum ring
to the end of the plain aluminum chain. To
create a Möbius ball, thread another small
red jump ring through the small aluminum
ring and the previous small red jump ring,
and close the ring. Repeat with a third small
red jump ring, threading it through both of
the previous red rings, and close. Add the
remaining two rings in the same manner.
Attach the lobster claw clasp to the opposite
end of the chain to complete the necklace.

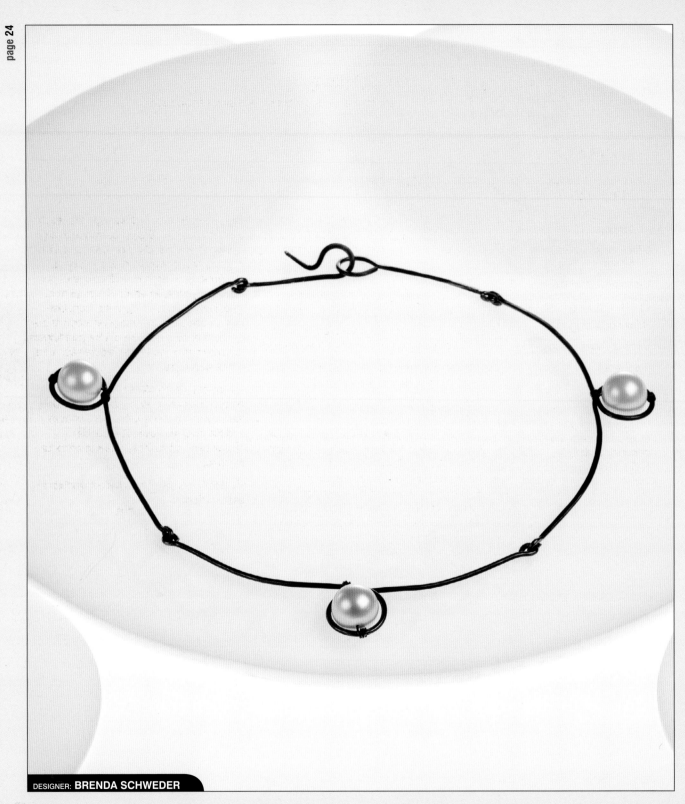

WIREWORK • HAMMERING • USING SEALING WAX

⫸ ▶ **Get Set**

Steel wire, 16 gauge,
    23 inches (58.4 cm)

Steel wire, 24 gauge,
    9 inches (22.9 cm)

3 ivory shell pearls, each
    12 mm

Clasp of your choice

Bench tool kit, page 9

Heavy-duty cutters

Sealing wax and rag

Steel wool

FINISHED SIZE
Necklace, 16 inches
(40.6 cm) with three
pendants, each ¾ x ¾ inch
(1.9 x 1.9 cm)

⫸ ▶ ▶ **Go**

1. Use the heavy-duty cutters to cut three lengths of the 16-gauge wire, each 7½ inches (19.1 cm). Bend the center of each length around a ⅝-inch (1.6 cm) mandrel, making a complete circle.

2. With the smallest part of the round-nose pliers, form a plain loop at both ends of each wire length. Use the flat-nose pliers to orient the loops perpendicular to two of the wires.

3. Use your fingers to curve each wire length to follow the curvature of a 6-inch (15.2 cm) circle. Texture each wire with a steel hammer.

4. Cut three lengths of 24-gauge wire, each 3 inches (7.6 cm). Thread and center a pearl on each length. Fit the threaded pearl into the circle formed in step 1, and wrap the ends of the wire around the center top and center bottom of the circle. Use flat-nose pliers to completely wrap the 24-gauge wire around the 16-gauge wire.

5. Cut two lengths of 16-gauge wire, each 3 inches (7.6 cm). Bend a ⅜-inch (9.5 mm) plain loop at the ends of both lengths with large round-nose pliers or forming pliers. Use flat-nose pliers to bend the end of one loop into a straight section ¼ inch (6 mm) long, leaving an opening in the loop. Use round-nose pliers to bend plain loops at the opposite ends of each wire. Use your fingers to gently curve each wire. Texture each wire with a steel hammer.

6. Lay out the necklace with the perpendicular-looped lengths at each side, the parallel-looped lengths at the bottom, and the clasp halves at the top. Use chain-nose and flat-nose pliers to connect the loops.

7. Gently rub the wire with steel wool and seal it with wax.

►► ► Get Set

Sterling silver cable chain,
2.5 x 3 mm, 17.8 cm

Sterling silver cable chain,
4 x 5 mm, 31.8 cm

Sterling silver half-hard
wire, 24 gauge, 45.7 cm

Rough topaz bead,
approximately 26 x 9 mm

3 sterling silver thick jump
rings, 6 mm

Sterling silver flattened
cable chain, 7 x 8 mm,
6.4 cm

Sterling silver cable chain,
5.5 x 7 mm, 2.5 cm
(approximately 3 links)

3 sterling silver thick jump
rings, 5 mm

3 rough topaz beads,
approximately 6 x 11 mm

Sterling silver lobster claw
clasp, 11 mm

Sterling silver soldered
jump ring, 9 mm

Bench tool kit, page 9

Liver of sulfur

FINISHED SIZE
Necklace, 46 cm

DESIGNER'S NOTE
Oxidize all of the sterling
silver components in a
liver-of-sulfur solution before beginning the project.

►► ► Go

1. Cut the 2.5 x 3-mm cable chain into
four sections: 1.3 cm, 3.2 cm, 4.4 cm, and
7.6 cm long.

2. Cut a 4.1-cm section of the 4 x 5-mm
cable chain. Cut the leftover piece into two
sections, each measuring 13.3 cm.

3. Cut 12.7 cm of the 24-gauge sterling
silver wire, and use this to make a wrapped
loop on either side of the large rough topaz
bead. Attach a 6-mm jump ring to one end of
the wire-wrapped bead.

4. Attach the following three chains to the
6-mm jump ring: the 7 x 8-mm flattened
cable chain; the 7.6-cm cable chain
(2.5 x 3 mm); and the 4.4-cm cable chain
(4 x 5 mm).

5. Attach a 6-mm jump ring to the other end
of the wire wrapped bead. Attach the three-
link section of the 5.5 x 7-mm cable chain to
this ring.

6. Using a 5-mm jump ring, link the three-
link section of the 5.5 x 7-mm cable chain to
a 13.3-cm piece of the 4 x 5-mm cable chain.
Half of the necklace is now complete.

7. Make a wire wrapped loop on one side of
a small topaz bead. Attach the short section
of the 4 x 5-mm cable chain to the loop.
Make a second wire wrapped loop the other
side of the bead and connect it to the 4.4-cm
length of the 2.5 x 3-mm cable chain.

8. Make a wire wrapped loop on one side
of the second small topaz bead, and attach
it to the flattened cable chain. Make a wire
wrapped loop on the other side of the bead
and attach it to the 3.2-cm length of the
2.5 x 3-mm cable chain.

9. Make a wire wrapped loop on one side of
the third small topaz bead and attach it to the
7.6-cm length of the 2.5 x 3-mm cable chain.
Make a wire wrapped loop on the other side
of the bead and attach it to the 1.3-cm length
of the 2.5 x 3-mm cable chain.

10. Gather the three free ends of 2.5 x 3-mm
cable chain and the remaining 13.3-cm length
of 4 x 5-mm cable chain. Connect these
chains with a 6-mm jump ring.

11. Use the remaining 5-mm jump rings to
attach the lobster claw clasp to one end of
the necklace and a 9-mm soldered jump ring
to other end.

12. If you would like to brighten the oxidized
silver, gently rub over the finished piece with
an abrasive pad.

Get Set

Sterling silver tubing,
  10 mm OD, 8.5 mm ID,
  2¼ inches (5.7 cm)

Two-part epoxy, quick
  drying

Purple powdered enamel

Leather cord with clasp,
  1 mm, 16 inches
  (40.6 cm)

Bench tool kit, page 9

Masking tape

Small plastic cup

Wooden craft stick

Sandpaper, 150 to 600 grit

Green nylon kitchen
  scrubber

FINISHED SIZE
Pendant, 2¼ x ⅜ inch
(5.7 x 0.95 cm)

DESIGNER'S NOTE
Many types of pigment,
such as tempera paint or
even ground makeup, can
be used to color epoxy.

Go

1. File the ends of the sterling silver tubing diagonally in the same direction, creating two angles, each with a hypotenuse of 10 mm. Sand the ends of the tube smooth.

2. Mark a point on each side of the tubing that is 4 mm from the top edge. At each marked point, drill a hole that is large enough to accommodate the leather cord.

3. Cover the bottom end of the tube with masking tape. Make sure the masking tape completely seals the end of the tube.

4. In the paper cup, mix the two-part epoxy according to the manufacturer's instructions. Add the pigment to the mixed epoxy. Be sure to work quickly so the epoxy does not begin to harden.

5. Use a wooden craft stick to transfer the colored epoxy into the top of the sealed tubing. Fill the tubing halfway. Let the epoxy completely cure, then remove the masking tape.

6. Begin sanding the epoxy with 150-grit sandpaper, and work your way through successive grits, finishing with 600-grit paper. Rub the silver tube with a green kitchen scrub for a matte finish. String the leather cord through the drilled holes.

⊳ ▶ **Get Set**

Brass sheet, 18 gauge,
    2 x 3 inches (5.1 cm x
    7.6 cm)

Brass tubing, 2.1 mm OD,
    1.6 mm ID, 2 inches
    (5.1 cm)

Brass rod, 14 gauge,
    2 inches (5.1 cm)

Black rubber cord necklace
    with clasp, 3 mm

Green patina

Antique black patina
    (for brass, copper, and
    bronze)

Bench tool kit, page 9

Acetylene torch

Paintbrush

Acetone

Spray lacquer or
    sealing wax

Cup burr, 2.5 mm

FINISHED SIZE
Pendant, 1¼ x 1¼ x ¼ inch
(3.2 x 3.2 x 0.6 cm)

▶ ▶ ▶ **Go**

1. Use dividers to mark two 1¼-inch (3.2 cm) disks on the brass sheet. Mark a ¾-inch (1.9 cm) circle in the center of one of the marked 1¼-inch (3.2 cm) disks. Use a jeweler's saw to cut out the disks. Pierce and saw out the interior circle marked on one disk. (This now resembles a washer.) File all cut metal edges.

2. On the brass "washer," mark four equidistant points, each ⅛ inch (3 mm) from the edge. Drill a 1.6-mm hole at each marked point.

3. Tape the brass disk and the washer together. Drill back through the four holes and through the solid brass disk. This ensures that the holes line up perfectly.

4. Use a saw to cut four 5-mm lengths of brass tube (rivet spacers) and four 10-mm lengths of brass rod (rivet wire). File and sand the ends flat on all eight pieces. Sand the disk and the washer with 220-grit sandpaper.

5. Warm the brass washer with a torch and then use a small brush to apply the green patina. Dip the brass disk into the antique black solution until it is completely black. Wipe the washer and the disk with acetone to remove any residue, and coat both metal pieces with spray lacquer or wax.

6. Place the blackened disk on a steel block. Thread one brass wire rivet through a brass tube spacer and through one hole in the blackened disk. Thread the top of the rivet wire through the corresponding hole in the green washer. Rivet this connection. Repeat this process to rivet the remaining three holes. Use a 2.5-mm cup burr to shape the rivet heads and to remove any sharp edges.

7. Slide the rubber cord between the two layers of the pendant, using a tube spacer as the bail.

►► Get Set

Leather, 1.5 mm thick, 8½ x 12 inches (21.6 x 30.5 cm)

2 small rapid rivets

Photocopied design template ❶, enlarged 400%

Craft glue

Cardstock, 8½ x 12 inches (21.6 x 30.5 cm)

Permanent marker

Paper scissors

Sewing shears

Rawhide mallet

Rotating leather punch or 4 leather or gasket punches, ⅛ inch (0.3 cm), ⁵⁄₃₂ inch (0.4 cm), ³⁄₁₆ inch (0.5 cm), and ⁷⁄₃₂ inch (0.6 cm) in diameter

Scrap piece of granite countertop

Steel bench block or small anvil

Rivet-setting tool

Craft knife

FINISHED SIZE
8 x 11 inches
(20.3 x 27.9 cm)

DESIGNER'S NOTES
You can make the necklace with either one piece of leather, 1.5 mm thick, or attach two pieces of garment leather to each other (wrong sides together) with leather glue.

Rivets have two components; the bottom, which has a base and an upright shaft, and the cap. The rivets won't be attached tightly against the leather; instead, you'll set them loosely to allow them to serve like buttons. The looseness is achieved by placing scraps of leather on the shaft to create a lot of space between the base and the cap, and removing the scraps after setting the cap.

❶

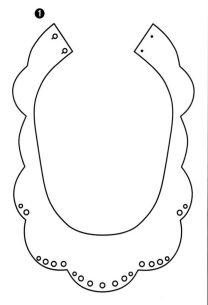

►►► Go

1. Trace the template onto the leather, then cut it out with the sewing shears.

2. Transfer the placement marks for the decorative holes from the template onto the leather. Punch out the holes using a ⁷⁄₃₂-inch (0.6 cm) punch for the large holes, and a ⁵⁄₃₂-inch (0.4 cm) punch for the small holes.

3. Transfer the two placement marks for the rivets from the template onto the leather. Punch a ⅛-inch (0.3 cm) hole at each spot. Set aside. Cut three scraps of leather, each approximately 1 inch (2.5 cm) square. Punch a ⅛-inch (0.3 cm) hole in each scrap near an edge, then cut from the edge to the hole. Set aside.

4. Place the piece of granite on your worktable, with the anvil atop it. Put the leather, right side up, over the anvil, with the rivet's shaft sticking up through one of the holes. Thread each of the scraps, one after the other, onto the shaft. Place the cap onto the end of the shaft. Hold the concave end of the rivet-setting tool against the cap and strike a firm blow with the mallet to set the rivet. Pull the scraps away from the rivet; since you cut from edge to hole, it should come away easily. Set the other rivet in the remaining hole, using the same method.

5. Transfer both of the placement marks for the fastening holes from the template onto the leather, and punch ³⁄₁₆-inch (0.5 cm) holes at those spots. On each, use a craft knife to make a tiny slit—no more than ⅛ inch (0.3 cm) long—facing away from the necklace edge, as shown on the template. Check to see if you can get the fastening holes over the rivets. If not, cut the slits longer, a tiny bit at a time, until the closing mechanism works.

▶▶ ▶ Get Set

Butterfly images of your choice or photocopied design template ❶, enlarged 133%

Red metallic paper, 8½ x 11 inches (21.6 x 27.9 cm)

Transparency sheet, 8½ x 11 inches (21.6 x 27.9 cm)

8 silver-color anodized brads, each ⅛ inch (3 mm)

Sterling silver flat cable chain, 1.5 mm, 11 inches (27.9 cm)

12 sterling silver jump rings, 20 gauge, each 5 mm

Sterling silver clasp, ½ inch (1.3 cm)

Bench tool kit, page 9

Computer scanner

Computer with photo editing software

Inkjet printer

Scissors

Single-hole punch, ¹⁄₁₆ inch (1.6 mm)

FINISHED SIZE
Necklace, 21 inches (53.3 cm) including drop pendant

▶ ▶ ▶ Go

1. Scan the photocopied design templates or butterfly images of your choice onto your computer. Using imaging software, copy and arrange eight butterfly designs on one page. Enlarge or reduce five butterflies to measure approximately 1¾ x 1½ inches (4.4 x 3.8 cm) and three to measure approximately 1½ x 1 inch (4 x 2.5 cm).

2. Print the butterfly designs onto both the red metallic paper and the transparency sheet. Cut out the printed butterfly shapes.

3. Tightly hold a transparent butterfly on top of a paper butterfly. Cut a hole in the middle of the layered butterflies with the hole punch. Repeat with each pair, making a total of eight sets of butterflies.

4. Punch a hole that is 3 mm from the top edge of both wings of seven paper butterflies. In one of these paper butterflies, punch a hole that is 3 mm from the bottom edge of the left wing. On the eight unpunched butterflies, punch a hole that is 3 mm from the edge of the right top wing.

5. Connect a transparent butterfly to a paper butterfly with a round silver brad through the center hole. Loop both sides of the back of each brad with round-nose pliers. Use your fingers to slightly offset the transparent butterflies.

6. Cut the chain into three sections: one 2½ inches (6.4 cm) long and two 4½ inches (11.4 cm) long.

7. Connect the seven butterflies together with jump rings, making sure the butterfly in the center is the one with the extra hole on the bottom wing.

8. Connect the butterfly with only one hole to the center butterfly, using jump rings and the 2½-inch (6.4 cm) chain. Connect the two 4½-inch (11.4 cm) sections of chain on each side of the butterflies with jump rings.

9. Attach the clasp with a jump ring and add one jump ring to the opposite end of the chain.

▶▶ Get Set

Sterling silver sheet,
20 gauge, 1 x 1½ inches
(2.5 x 3.8 cm)

Sterling silver spring-ring
clasp, 5 mm

Sterling silver cable chain,
1.5 mm, 15.5 inches
(38.5 cm)

Sterling silver jump ring,
20 gauge, 5 mm

Sterling silver end tag,
24 gauge, 7 x 4 mm

Sterling silver jump ring,
18 gauge, 7 mm

Photocopied design
templates ❶

Glue stick

Bench tool kit, page 9

Ball burr, 1.2 mm

Sandpaper, 180 and
320 grit

Liver of sulfur

FINISHED SIZE
Pendant, ⅝ x ½ inch
(1.6 x 1.3 cm)

▶▶▶ Go

1. Glue the photocopied design templates onto the sterling silver sheet, making sure the templates adhere well.

2. Use a scribe to indent the metal where the holes will be drilled. Drill the metal with a 0.8-mm bit. Enlarge the drilled holes with a 1.2-mm ball burr.

3. With a jeweler's saw, cut out the three cloud forms from the sterling silver sheet. Remove the paper templates. File and sand each silver cloud with 320-grit and 400-grit sandpaper.

❶

4. To create a crisscross finish, sand both sides of the largest silver cloud in random directions with 180-grit sandpaper.

5. Patina the two smallest silver clouds with a liver-of-sulfur solution. Rinse the small metal clouds and let dry.

6. Brush both sides of the smallest silver clouds with a green kitchen scrub pad until the silver color shows through the patina.

7. Attach the clasp to one end of the chain. Attach the 5-mm jump ring to the other end of the chain and to the end tag.

8. From smallest to largest, assemble the silver clouds on the 7-mm jump ring. Attach the jump ring to the chain and close.

SAWING • DRILLING • FILING • SANDING

▶▶ Get Set

Sterling silver sheet,
    18 gauge, 2½ x 4 inches
    (6.4 x 10.2 cm)

Plastic-covered steel wire,
    0.38 mm, 39½ inches
    (100 cm)

Sterling silver tube,
    1.5 mm, ⁷⁄₁₆ inch (1 cm)

Photocopied design
    template ❶

Bench tool kit, page 9

FINISHED SIZE
Pendant, 2½ x 3¼ x 4
inches (6.4 x 8.3 x 10.2 cm)

▶▶▶ Go

1. Transfer the photocopied design template onto the 18-gauge sterling silver sheet, and saw out the design. Drill the hole at the top of the bird's body using a 1-mm bit.

2. File and sand the edges of the metal smooth. With steel wool or 400-grit sandpaper, rub each silver surface in a circular motion.

3. Fit the sawed slits on the silver wings together. Slide the cross of the wings into the slit cut into the body shape, making sure the wings are facing in the appropriate direction.

4. Cut the steel wire with snips. Thread the bird onto the steel wire and loop the wire back through the hole to make the bail and secure the bird in one place on the wire.

5. Slide the steel wire ends into the silver tube, making sure the ends overlap inside the tube. Use round-nose pliers to press the tube together in two equidistant places to secure the steel wire.

❶
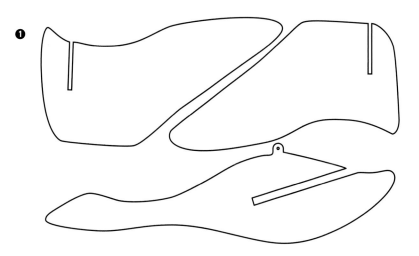

▶▶ **Get Set**

2 small, drilled river stones, each ½ to ¾ inch (1.3 to 1.9 cm)

Sterling silver cable chain, 6 x 9 mm, 3 links

2 sterling silver jump rings, 18 gauge, each 6 mm

2 faceted sapphire rondelles, each 4 mm

2 sterling silver headpins, 26 gauge, each 2½ inches (6.4 cm)

Sterling silver cable chain, 1.5 x 2 mm, 16 inches (40.6 cm)

Sterling silver lobster claw clasp, 9 mm

Sterling silver soldered jump ring, 18 gauge, 7 mm

2 sterling silver jump rings, 18 gauge, each 4 mm

Bench tool kit, page 9

Liver of sulfur

FINISHED SIZE
Pendant, 1½ x ½ inch (3.8 x 1.3 cm)

▶▶▶ **Go**

1. Use a liver-of-sulfur solution to oxidize all sterling silver materials.

2. Use chain-nose and flat-nose pliers to attach one river rock to the bottom link of the three-link cable chain using a 6-mm jump ring. Attach the second river rock to the top link with the remaining 6-mm jump ring.

3. Thread a sapphire rondelle onto each headpin. Make two wire wrapped loops attaching one sapphire to the top link of the three link section of cable chain and the second sapphire to the middle link.

4. String the top link of the three-link cable chain onto the 16-inch (40.6 cm) section of small cable chain.

5. Using flat-nose and round-nose pliers, attach the 9-mm lobster claw and 7-mm soldered jump ring to either end of the 16-inch (40.6 cm) cable chain with the 4-mm jump rings.

6. To brighten the oxidized silver, gently rub steel wool over the finished necklace.

**PIERCING · SAWING · FILING · DAPPING
FORMING · BALLING WIRE · RIVETING · POLISHING**

▶ ▶ **Get Set**

Sterling silver sheet,
   22 gauge, 3 x 6 inches
   (7.6 x 15.2 cm)

Sterling silver round wire,
   18 gauge, ½ inch
   (1.3 cm)

Black onyx round bead,
   4 mm

Sterling silver snake chain,
   2.5 mm, 16 or 18 inches
   (40.6 or 45.7 cm)

Photocopied design
   template ❶, enlarged
   133%

Bench tool kit, page 9

Scissors

Glue stick

Cross-locking tweezers

Torch

FINISHED SIZE
Pendant, 3¼ x 2½ inches
(8.3 x 6.4 cm)

▶ ▶ ▶ **Go**

1. Cut out the photocopied template and glue it to the silver sheet.

2. Center punch and drill holes for the interior cutouts and the rivet hole. Using a jeweler's saw, cut out the interior shapes first, and then the exterior pattern. Remove the template and glue from the silver shape. Smooth all cut edges with a half-round file.

3. Place the narrow, curved end of the silver shape in a dapping block. Dome this area with a punch and a hammer. Polish the silver shape.

4. Using chain-nose pliers, bend the domed end of the piece through the center opening. Shape the rest of the pendant with your fingers.

5. Use a torch to ball one end of the 18-gauge round wire. With the balled end on the front, thread the wire through the onyx bead and the pendant. Trim the wire so ⅟₁₆ inch (1.6 mm) remains. Use a riveting hammer to carefully tap the end of the wire, spreading the top.

6. Polish the pendant with rouge compound and slide on the chain.

❶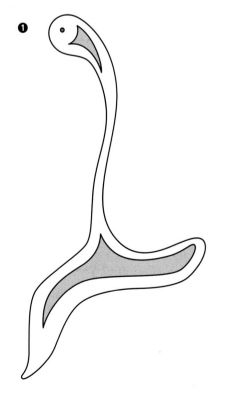

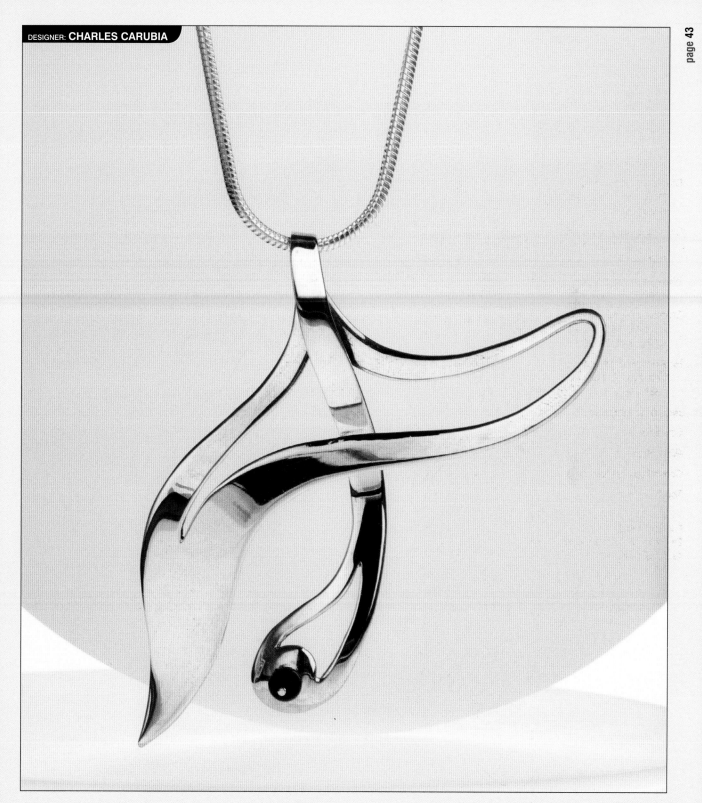

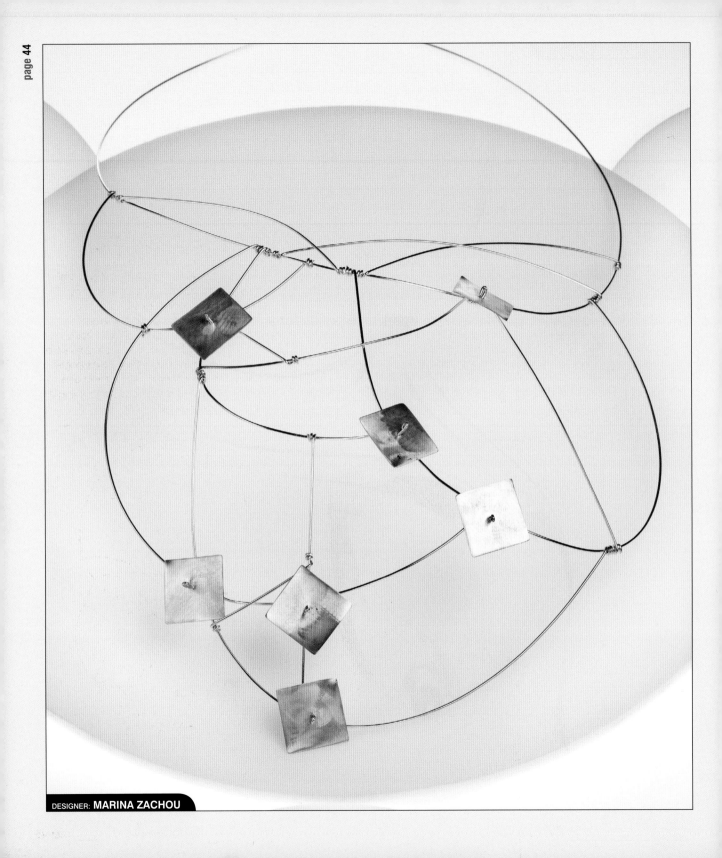

DESIGNER: **MARINA ZACHOU**

▶▶ Get Set

Sterling silver wire,
    18 gauge, 100 inches
    (2.5 m)

7 sterling silver squares,
    24 gauge, each ¾ x ¾
    inch (1.9 x 1.9 cm)

Photocopied design
    template **❶**, enlarged
    400%

Bench tool kit, page 9

FINISHED SIZE
Necklace, 8 x 13 inches
(20.3 x 33 cm)

▶▶▶ Go

1. Use snips to cut a 24-inch (61 cm) length of the 18-gauge silver wire. Using round-nose pliers, make a loop on one end of the wire. On the other wire end, make a small hook that is approximately ½ inch (1.3 cm) long. Form this length into a neck wire that is 7 inches (17.8 cm) in diameter.

2. Mark and drill the center of each sterling silver square with a 1-mm bit. Sand the edges and the surface of each square with 400-grit sandpaper.

3. Position the neck wire on your work surface with the clasp at the top. Following the enlarged design template, cut and add lengths of the sterling silver wire and the silver squares to the neck wire. For each connection, wrap the tails of each wire around the connecting wire three or four times. When adding a silver square, leave the tail of the wrapped connection 7 mm longer. Thread the silver square onto the wire and use round-nose pliers to bend the wire into a U shape, securing the square.

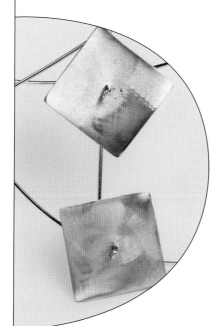

❶

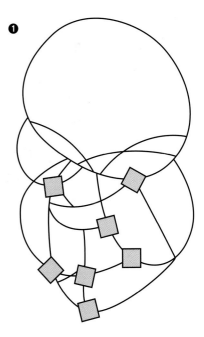

▶▶ Get Set

Sterling silver sheet,
18 gauge, 1 x 1½ inches
(2.5 x 3.8 cm), annealed
and polished

Leather cord, 1.5 mm,
29 inches (73.7 cm)

Paper punch for making a
patterned border

Heavyweight paper

Bench tool kit, page 9

Rolling mill

Clear tape

Marker

FINISHED SIZE
Pendant, ¾ x 1½ inches
(1.9 x 3.8 cm)

▶▶▶ Go

1. Using the paper punch, punch the patterned border design in the heavy-weight paper.

2. Center the punched paper design on the polished front surface of the sterling silver sheet. Place a plain piece of the same heavyweight paper behind the metal, sandwiching the silver sheet between the two paper pieces. Adjust the rollers of the rolling mill so the paper and metal stack is slightly too thick to fit between them. Roll the paper and metal stack through the rolling mill.

3. Apply clear tape to the front surface of the silver sheet to protect it.

4. Use a marker to draw a ¾ x 1½-inch (1.9 x 3.8 cm) rectangle on the embossed metal. Center the rectangle on the embossed pattern and curve the top and bottom ends. This is the shape of the pendant.

5. Draw a small horizontal rectangle near the top end of the pendant. This rectangle must be large enough to accommodate the leather cord. Pierce and saw out the small rectangle, and file the edges smooth.

6. Saw out the larger pendant shape. File, sand, and polish its edges.

7. Loop the leather cord and insert it through the rectangular hole near the top of the pendant. Thread the tail back through the loop, securing the leather cord to the pendant. Tie a simple knot at the ends of the cord to secure the necklace.

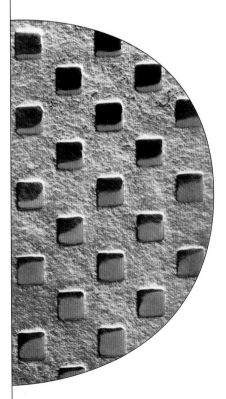

▶ Get Ready

WIREWORK • USING PHOTO EDITING SOFTWARE
SCANNING • PRINTING • DRILLING • GLUING

▶▶ Get Set

2 sheets shrinkable
   thermoplastic for inkjet
   printers

Gold-plated curb chain,
   5 mm, 1 inch (2.5 cm)

4 pair black sew-on snaps,
   size 3/0

Gold-plated curb chain,
   2 mm, 24 inches (61 cm)

4 gold-plated jump rings,
   18 gauge, each 8 mm

Snips

Scanner

Computer with photo
   editing software

Inkjet printer

Scissors

Hole punch

Oven or toaster oven

Baking sheet

Flexible shaft

Drill bit, 3 mm

Two-part epoxy for metal
   and plastic

Chain-nose pliers

FINISHED SIZE
Chain, 36 inches
(91.4 cm); each pendant,
6 x ¾ inch
(15.2 x 1.9 cm)

▶▶▶ Go

1. Snip three links of the 5-mm curb chain. Lay the chain flat on the scanner. Scan the segment into a photo-editing program. Crop the image so that the chain segment takes up the entire frame. Enlarge the chain image to 5½ x 1½ inches (14 x 3.8 cm).

2. Create a new 8 x 10-inch (20.3 x 25.4 cm) document. Copy and paste the chain image into the new document. Copy and paste it two more times for a total of three separate chain images aligned side by side in the new document. Adjust the image brightness level, making the document 50 percent lighter.

3. Following the manufacturer's instructions, load the shrinkable thermoplastic sheets into the printer. Print the document with the chain images two times. You now have a six printed chain segments.

4. Cut out each of the printed chain segments with scissors, following the curves of the images. Punch a centered hole in one end of four of the chain segments, 4 mm in from the edge.

VARIATION

5. Following the shrinkable thermoplastic sheet instructions, bake the printed chain segments on a baking sheet in an oven. Let the segments cool.

6. Select two of the punched plastic segments and place their printed surface up. On the end opposite the punched hole, measure and mark a centered point that is 6 mm in from one end. Drill a hole that goes only halfway through the sheet at the marked point. Use epoxy to adhere a female half of a snap into the partially drilled hole.

7. Place the two remaining punched plastic segments with the non-printed surface facing up. Use epoxy to adhere a male half of a snap on the end opposite the punched hole.

8. On the printed surface of the two non-punched plastic segments, measure and mark a centered point that is 6 mm in from one end. Drill a hole that goes only halfway through the sheet at the marked point. Use epoxy to adhere a female half of a snap into the partially drilled hole. Turn the segments over. Use epoxy to adhere a male half of a snap on the opposite end.

9. Divide the plastic segments into two matching groups. Each group should have three segments: one punched with a female half of a snap, one punched with a male half of a snap, and one un-punched with half of a snap on each end. Snap the segments together, creating two sections of plastic chains, each with holes at the ends.

10. Cut the 2-mm curb chain into two lengths, 14 inches (35.6 cm) and 10 inches (25.4 cm). Attach the chain to the plastic sections with jump rings.

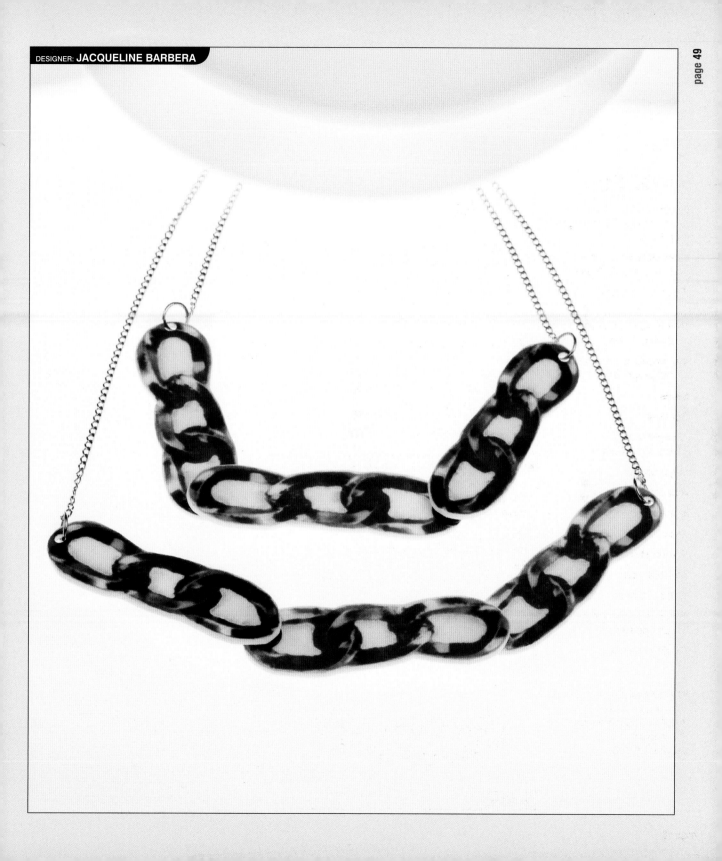

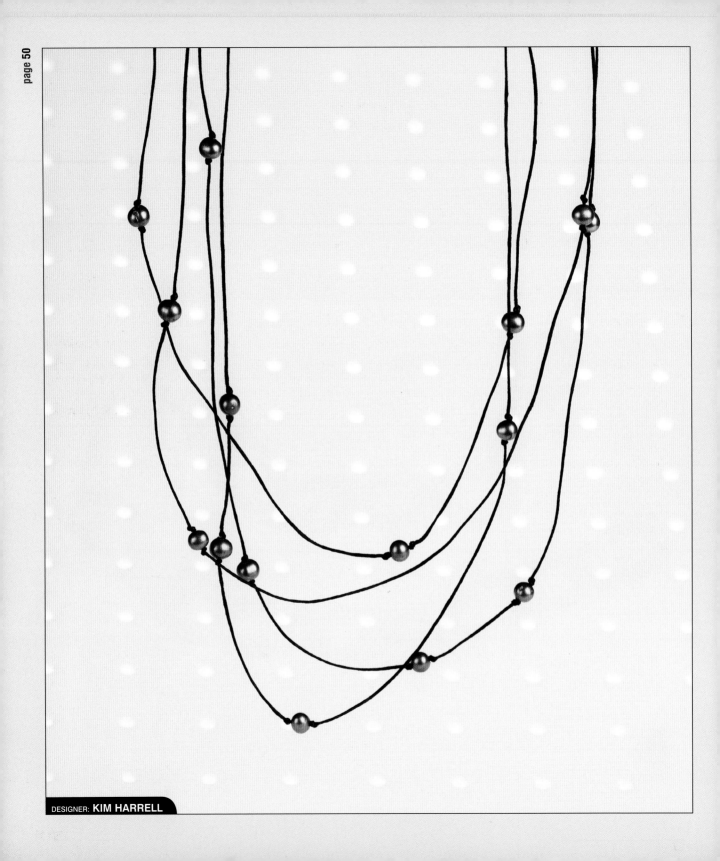

→ Get Ready

▶▶ Get Set

Black waxed linen cord, 200 inches (508 cm)

24 green-gold pearls, each ¼ inch (6 mm) in diameter

Fine silver tube, 2 mm OD, ½ inch (1.3 cm)

Liver of sulfur

Epoxy

Bench tool kit, page 9

Broaching pin, optional

Knotting tool

FINISHED SIZE
Necklace, 108 inches (2.7 m)

DESIGNER'S NOTE
Wrap the necklace around your neck as many or as few times as you like.
.

▶▶▶ Go

1. Secure one end of the waxed linen cord in a vise so the cord is taut.

2. Tie a knot in the cord about 6 inches (15.2 cm) away from the vise, string one pearl onto the cord, and push it to meet the knot. Tip: If necessary, use a broaching pin to ream out the pearls so they fit on the cord.

3. Start another knot as close to the pearl as possible and use the knotting tool to glide the loop of the knot flush to the pearl.

4. Repeat Step 2, staggering the space between the pearls and creating a few bunches of two or three pearls close together until you have used all 24 pearls.

5. File the ends of the fine silver tube smooth. Oxidize the tube in a liver-of-sulfur solution. Make sure the inside and outside of the tube is completely dry.

6. Place a small amount of epoxy into both ends of the tube, and insert one end of the linen cord into each side of the tube. Let the epoxy dry.

▶ ▶ Get Set

Sterling silver cable chain, 4 x 5 mm, 12½ inches (31.8 cm)

Sterling silver hammered cable chain, 5 x 7 mm, 4 inches (10.2 cm)

Sterling silver cable chain, 2.5 x 3 mm, 6½ inches (16.5 cm)

Sterling silver half-hard round wire, 24 gauge, 12 inches (30.5 cm)

Sterling silver half-hard round wire, 26 gauge, 18 inches (45.7 cm)

3 red sapphire faceted beads, each 5 mm

Sterling silver wire chaos bead, 11 mm

Moss amethyst faceted nugget bead, 9 x 12 mm

Sterling silver lobster claw clasp, 11 mm

Sterling silver soldered jump ring, 9 mm

2 sterling silver jump rings, each 5 mm

Liver of sulfur

Bench tool kit, page 9

Green nylon kitchen scrubber

FINISHED SIZE
Necklace, 18 inches (45.7 cm)

▶ ▶ ▶ Go

1. Oxidize all sterling silver components using a liver-of-sulfur solution.

2. Use snips to cut the 4 x 5-mm cable chain into two sections, each measuring 6 inches (15.2 cm). Cut the hammered chain into two sections, one measuring 2½ inches (6.4 cm) or 12 links long, and the other measuring 1 inch (2.5 cm) or 4 links long. Cut four pieces of the 2.5 x 3-mm cable chain into three sections: two pieces each measuring 1⅝ inches (4.1 cm), one measuring 1 inch (2.5 cm), and the fourth piece measuring 2⁷⁄₁₆ inches (6.1 cm).

3. Use snips to cut the 24-gauge and 26-gauge wire into 6-inch (15.2 cm) sections. With your round-nose pliers, make a loop near the end of each wire. Leave the tail free for now.

4. Thread a sapphire bead onto each of the three 26-gauge sections, and the larger beads onto each of the 24-gauge sections. Make an open loop on the other side of each bead, leaving the tail free.

5. Attach the wire with a sapphire bead in the middle of the hammered chain sections and close the loops by wrapping the tails around the bottom of the loop two to three times. Snip off any extra wire. Attach another wire with a sapphire bead in the middle of the small cable chain sections measuring 1⅝ inches (4.1 cm) and 1 inch (2.5 cm) and close the loops. Attach the final sapphire bead in the middle of the remaining cable chain and close the loops.

6. Attach the section of wire with the wire chaos bead to one length of the larger cable chain and close the loop. Make another loop on the other side of the bead and attach the three lengths of chain with the sapphire beads, making sure the beads are spaced evenly. Repeat this with the moss agate bead and the remaining chain, threading the three smaller lengths of chain on the loop in the same order as the other side.

7. Using your flat-nose and chain-nose pliers, attach the lobster claw and soldered jump ring to either end of the necklace with the 5-mm jump rings.

8. Gently rub the green kitchen scrubber over your finished piece for a slightly brighter finish.

→ Get Ready

WIREWORK • HAMMERING • FORMING WITH A MANDREL • USING SEALING WAX

▶ ▶ Get Set

Steel wire, 16 gauge, 31 inches (78.7 cm)

Steel wire, 19 gauge, 10 inches (25.4 cm)

Clasp of your choice

2 jet hematite–colored crystal beads, each 8 mm

Black diamond–colored crystal bead, 8 mm

2 black diamond–colored crystal beads, each 6 mm

Bench tool kit, page 9

Mandrel, 1 inch (2.5 cm)

Heavy-duty cutters

Sealing wax and rag

FINISHED SIZE
Necklace, 16 inches (40.6 cm); pendant, 1¼ x 5 inches (3.2 x 12.7 cm)

▶ ▶ ▶ Go

1. Cut five pieces of 16-gauge wire in the following lengths: 2½ inches (6.4 cm), 3 inches (7.6 cm), 3½ inches (8.9 cm), 4 inches (10.2 cm), and 4½ inches (11.4 cm).

2. Bend a ¼-inch (0.6 cm) loop at the end of each wire length with large round-nose or forming pliers. Bend a small plain loop at the opposite end of each of the five lengths with round-nose pliers. Use your fingers to bend a slight curve in each length. Texture each length with a steel hammer. Orient each small loop perpendicular to the large loop.

3. Use the heavy-duty cutters to cut a 3½-inch (8.9 cm) length of 16-gauge wire. Form this wire into a ring around a 1-inch (2.5 cm) mandrel. Use a hammer to texture the wire.

4. Cut four 4-inch (10.2 cm) lengths of 16-gauge steel wire. Form small plain loops

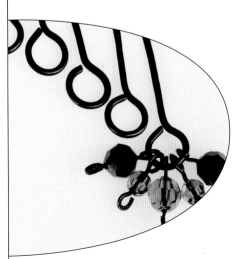

at each end of each wire length with round-nose pliers. Use your fingers to bend each wire into a curve corresponding with a 6-inch (15.2 cm) circle. Use a hammer to texture each length.

5. Use heavy-duty cutters to cut a 2-inch (5.1 cm) length of 16-gauge wire. Form a small plain loop with the smallest part of the round-nose pliers at one end of the length and a large plain loop with the largest part of the round-nose pliers at the remaining end. Bend the end of the large loop flat with flat-nose pliers. Texture the wire with a steel hammer.

6. Lay out the 4-inch (10.2-cm) wire lengths to form each side of the necklace. Position the ring at the bottom and the clasp hook at the top. Adjust the small loops so that the connections are perpendicular to each other, and use flat-nose and chain-nose pliers to connect the loops on each side of the necklace. Do not connect the center loops.

7. Open the 1-inch (2.5 cm) wire ring and add the curved components in increasing size, from left to right. Add the left and right necklace lengths to each side, and close the ring. Seal the necklace with wax.

8. Cut five lengths of 19-gauge wire, each 2 inches (5.1 cm). Form a plain loop at one end of each length with round-nose pliers. Texture each loop with a hammer and seal each wire with wax. Thread one bead on each length and form another plain loop on the remaining end with round-nose pliers. Open the large loop of the longest curved component, add the five crystal components, and close the loop with chain-nose pliers.

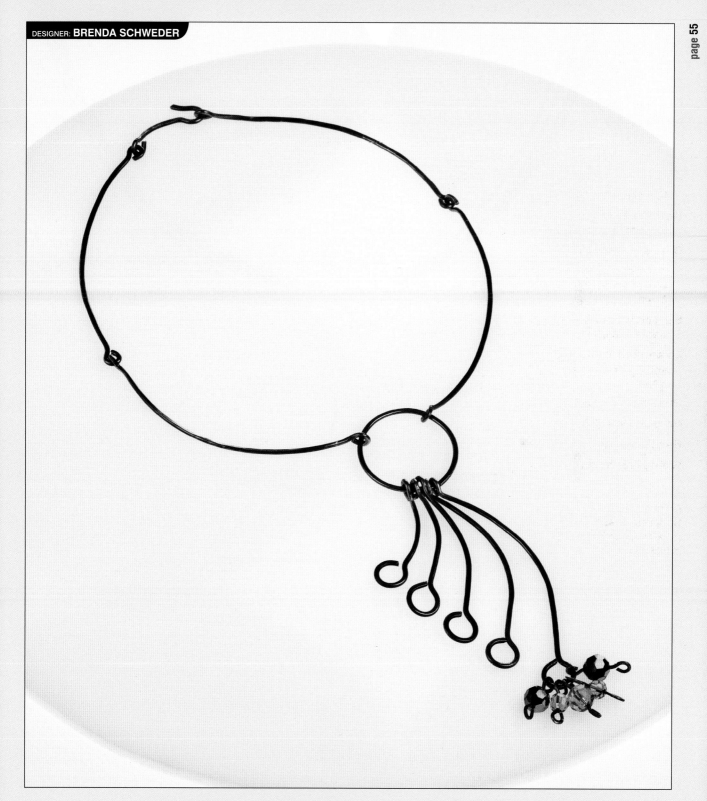

DESIGNER: **ISABELLE LAMONTAGNE**

►► Get Set

Sterling silver round wire,
    4 gauge, 1¼ inches
    (3.2 cm)

Sterling silver tubing,
    6.4 mm OD, 4 mm ID,
    1 inch (2.5 cm)

3 sterling silver round
    wires, 10 gauge, each
    ¾ inch (1.9 cm)

Black five-strand cable
    neck wire, 16 inches
    (40.6 cm)

Bench tool kit, page 9

Steel wool

Epoxy

FINISHED SIZE
Pendant, 1¼ x ¾ inch
(3.2 x 1.9 cm)

►►► Go

1. Measure and mark a point that is 2.5 mm from the top of the 4-gauge sterling silver wire. Drill a 2-mm hole at this point.

2. Insert the 4-gauge wire in the tube so the wire sticks out 5 mm from one end of the tube. Measure and mark points that are 6.6 mm, 13 mm, and 19.3 mm from the top of the tube. Drill holes at the marked points with a 3-mm bit.

3. Use rough sandpaper to create texture on the wire and polish the others parts with steel wool.

4. Slide the tube back onto the wire, align the holes, and insert one ¾ inch (1.9 cm) silver wire into each hole. Use epoxy to secure the wires in place.

5. Slide the black five-strand cable wire through the hole at the top of the wire.

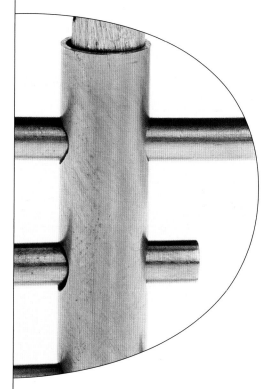

▶▶ ▶ Get Set

Moldable clay or dough,
    15-mm ball

Metal clay, 18 grams

Metal clay paste (slip)

Fine silver wire, 20 gauge,
    21 mm

Omega neck wire, 1.5 mm,
    18 inches (45.7 cm)

Playing cards

Lubricating balm or olive oil

Craft knife

Clay shaper

Food dehydrator

Rolling pin

Dowel or straw, 8 mm

Nonstick surface

Mini spatula

Torch

Sandpaper, 220, 400, 600,
    and 1200 grit

Brass brush

Agate burnisher

FINISHED SIZE
Necklace, 18 inches
(45.7 cm); pendant,
1¾ x 1¼ x ⅜ inch
(4.4 x 3.2 x 1.0 cm)

▶ ▶ ▶ Go

1. To make the armature, roll the ball of clay or dough into a 5½-inch-long (14 cm) log tapered at both ends. Bend the log into a U shape and place it on a card for easy transportation. Flatten the center slightly, making sure to maintain the U shape.

2. Roll out the metal clay to 1 mm (four cards) thick and 2½ x 2¾ inches (6.4 x 7 cm). Rub a small amount of lubricating balm or olive oil on the armature. Place the metal clay sheet over the armature. Trim off the excess metal clay and use a clay shaper to refine the shape. Let the metal clay dry for five minutes in a food dehydrator. Remove the pendant from the armature and continue to let it dry for five more minutes or until the metal clay is leather-hard.

3. Roll out the metal clay two cards thick. Cut a strip of metal clay that is ³⁄₁₆ x 1¼ inches (0.5 x 3.2 cm), and wrap it around a lightly greased straw or dowel. Secure the seams with a little slip, remove the excess clay, and dry the tube in the dehydrator.

4. Spread a small amount of paste clay (slip) on a nonstick surface with a mini spatula to make very thin texture sheets. Let the sheets dry.

5. Cut seven 1- to 3-mm pieces of fine silver wire. Melt the wires with a torch to make seven small silver balls of various sizes.

6. Remove the dry pendant from the dehydrator. Sand the pendant with progressively finer sandpaper, beginning with 220 grit and ending with 1200 grit. Remove any particularly rough surfaces on the top right side. Save the metal clay filings.

7. Break the thin texture sheets of metal clay into smaller pieces. Brush slip over the right half of the pendant. Sprinkle the thin clay sheets and some of the filings onto the pendant. Press gently to adhere the sprinkled pieces to the metal clay pendant. Brush this area with slip and make sure there are no sharp edges. Brush more slip in a few spots on the right side of the pendant, add the fine silver balls to those areas, and secure with slip. Let the pendant dry in the dehydrator.

8. With a craft knife, cut the tube made in Step 3 in half. File the edges of the tube. Turn the pendant over, and use slip to attach one piece of tube to the top recessed area on each side of the U shape. Clean up any excess clay with a clay shaper. Let the pendant dry in the dehydrator.

9. Place the pendant on a fire-resistant surface and torch fire the piece for five minutes. Air cool.

10. Brass-brush the entire pendant and burnish the high points with an agate burnisher. Thread the pendant onto the neck wire.

▶▶ Get Set

Copper sheet, 18 gauge,
9 x 9 inches
(22.9 x 22.9 cm)

Photocopied design
template ❶, enlarged
400%

Bench tool kit, page 9

Permanent marker

Steel wool

2-liter soft drink bottle

Liver of sulfur

FINISHED SIZE
7½ inches (19 cm) in
diameter, 1½ inches
(3.8 cm) wide

▶▶▶ Go

1. Adhere the photocopied design template to the copper sheet. Use a jeweler's saw to cut out the neckpiece. Remove the paper template. File and sand the cut metal edges.

2. With a fine-point permanent marker, draw the S-shape design onto the neckpiece. Drill a hole at one end of the S design. Insert a saw blade through the drilled hole and, following the marked line, saw the design.

3. Scrub the neckpiece with steel wool to remove unwanted scratches.

4. Lay a 2-liter soda bottle on its side. Place the neckpiece on the bottle and shape and curve the metal by hand.

5. From underneath, push the round parts of the S-shape design up to add dimension to the neckpiece.

6. Clean and degrease the copper. "Wash" the neckpiece with a weak solution of liver of sulfur—do not soak it. When the desired color is reached, rinse the neckpiece well with cold running water.

❶

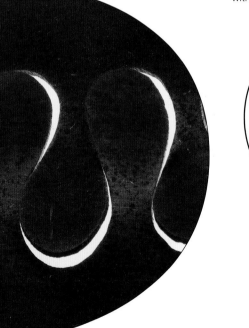

Get Ready

PIERCING · SAWING · FILING · SANDING · DRILLING · RIVETING

▶▶ **Get Set**

Yellow anodized aluminum sheet, 18 gauge, 2¼ x 1¾ inches (5.7 x 4.4 cm)

Red anodized aluminum sheet, 18 gauge, 2 x 1 inch (5.1 x 2.5 cm)

Brass wire, 20 gauge, 3 to 5 cm

Waxed cord, 1 mm, 30 inches (76.2 cm)

Photocopied design template ❶ and ❷

Bench tool kit, page 9

FINISHED SIZE
Pendant, 1¾ x 2½ inches (4.4 x 6.4 cm)

▶▶▶ **Go**

1. Transfer the photocopied design templates onto the red and yellow anodized aluminum sheets. Pierce and saw out the transferred designs, then file and sand the edges smooth.

2. Following the design template, mark and drill two 0.8-mm holes on the red aluminum shape. Position the red aluminum shape underneath the yellow aluminum shape. Using the 0.8-mm holes in the red shape as a guide, mark and drill two holes in the yellow aluminum.

3. Feed a length of 20-gauge wire through the holes in the aluminum layers drilled in step 2. Snip both wires so each end extends about 0.75 mm past each side of the layered aluminum. Rivet the wires.

4. Form the center of the 1-mm cord into a U shape, and thread it through the top of the sawed spiral on the yellow aluminum. Thread the tails of the cord through the U, and pull the cord tight. Tie a simple knot with the ends of the cord.

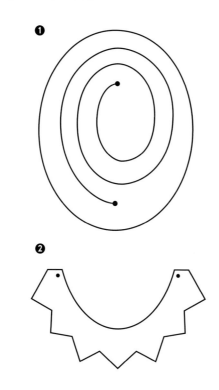

**SAWING • PIERCING • DRILLING • APPLYING GOLD LEAF • SANDING
WIREWORK • TIN SOLDERING • ADDING A PATINA**

▶▶ ▶ Get Set

Slate slab, 4 mm thick,
2 ¾ x 2 ¾ inches
(7 x 7 cm)

Gold leaf adhesive,
quick drying

Gold leaf, one sheet

Steel wire, 18 gauge,
8 inches (20.3 cm)

Hemp string, 32 inches
(81.3 cm)

Bench tool kit, page 9

Small paintbrush

Tin solder and flux

Soldering iron

Black oxide for steel

DESIGNER'S NOTES

Black oxide is also known
as "gun blue." This chemi-
cal creates a black oxide on
steel, similar to how liver of
sulfur darkens silver.

The cage in the center
of the pendant can hold
a piece of paper with a
mantra or a small letter
written on it or just hold a
note to help you remember
something.

▶▶ ▶ Go

1. Use calipers to draw a 2½-inch (6.4 cm) diameter circle on the piece of slate. Draw a second circle in the center of the first with a ¾-inch (1.9 cm) diameter. Use a scribe to mark eight equidistant points around the inner circle, 3 mm from the edge.

2. Use a saw to cut out the outer circle. Pierce and saw out the inner circle. Drill eight holes at the marked points around the inner circle.

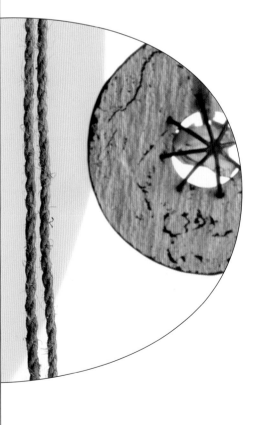

3. With a paintbrush, apply the gold leaf adhesive to one side of the slate disk. Adhere the gold leaf to the disk, and let it air dry. Wipe off the excess gold leaf with a soft cloth and sand the edges of the disk.

4. Wind the steel wire around a ⅞-inch-diameter (2.2 cm) mandrel six times. Cut off eight wire pieces from the coil, each slightly more than half a circle in length. Tip: To make each arc the same length, use the first piece of wire as a measuring guide for the other seven pieces.

5. Thread the eight half-circles of steel wire into the holes drilled in the slate disk. One by one, solder the wire ends together on one side of the disk with tin solder. Adjust the wires on the other side to form a sphere. Make sure all the wire ends are touching and solder the wires together at one time.

6. Blacken the steel wire with the black oxide. Rinse and dry the pendant. Thread the hemp string through the center of the pendant and tie a knot 1 inch (2.5 cm) from the end.

SAWING • HAMMERING • DRILLING • FILING • SANDING • SOLDERING
DAPPING • WIREWORK • ADDING A PATINA • BURNISHING

▶▶ ▶ Get Set

Sterling silver sheet,
  20 gauge, 1 x 1 inch
  (2.5 x 2.5 cm)

Brass wire, 22 gauge,
  6 inches (15.2 cm)

Sterling silver tubing, 4 mm
  OD, ¼ inch (6 mm)

Sterling silver wire,
  20 gauge, 2 inches
  (5.1 cm)

Sterling silver chain,
  18 inches (45.7 cm)

3 sterling silver jump rings,
  20 gauge, each 4 mm

Bench tool kit, page 9

Soldering kit, page 9

Concrete surface

Liver of sulfur

Sandpaper, 800 grit

FINISHED SIZE
Pendant, approximately
1 x 1 inch (2.5 x 2.5 cm)

▶▶ ▶ Go

1. Use a scribe to draw a heart shape on the silver sheet that measures approximately 1 inch (2.5 cm). Cut out the heart shape with a jeweler's saw.

2. Place the silver heart face down on a piece of concrete. Hammer the back of the metal until you achieve a texture that you like.

3. Draw a vertical line down the center of the silver heart with a scribe. Mark and drill three 1.75-mm holes on both sides of the line for the brass wire lacing. File and sand each drilled hole.

4. Saw the textured heart in half. File and sand the edges of each piece smooth.

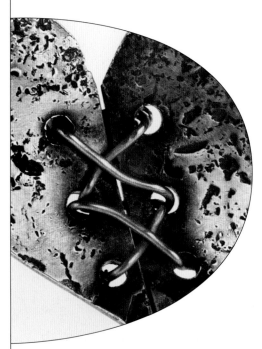

5. Position the silver pieces upside down and side by side on your work surface, creating the heart shape. Thread the brass wire through the bottom left hole from behind, leaving a small U-shaped tail. Making sure the wire is taut, lace it across to the center right hole. Continue lacing the wire through the remaining holes until there are two crosses on the front of the heart. Snip the brass wire tail to 4 mm, bend it to a U shape, and lightly hammer both wire ends flush with the back of the pendant.

6. Solder each end of the brass wire to the back of the pendant. File and sand any rough spots.

7. Place the pendant right side up in a large dapping hole. Use a large dapping punch to slightly curve the pendant.

8. Use a jeweler's saw to cut a 6-mm sterling silver tube to use for the bail. File and sand the cut edges. Solder the tube horizontally on the back of the heart near the top of the vertical cut.

9. With the tips of the round-nose pliers, bend the sterling silver wire into an S clasp. Place the clasp on a bench block, and hammer both inside curves of the clasp flat. Apply a liver-of-sulfur patina to the chain, clasp, jump rings, and pendant.

10. Use 800-grit sandpaper to remove most of the patina from the front of the pendant, leaving dark gray in the recessed areas. Burnish the edges of the pendant. String the pendant on the chain and attach the clasp to the chain with a jump ring. Attach two jump rings to the opposite end of the chain.

DESIGNER: **ERICA STANKWYTCH BAILEY**

➤ **Get Ready**

WIREWORK • FILING • FORGING • SWEAT SOLDERING
USING A ROLLING MILL • ANNEALING • FORMING • SANDING

▶ ▶ **Get Set**

3 brass or copper wires,
    16 gauge, each 1 inch
    (2.5 cm)

Sterling silver sheet,
    20 gauge, 1 x 2 inches
    (2.5 x 5.1 cm)

Snake chain with clasp,
    1.2 mm, 18 inches
    (40.6 cm)

Bench tool kit, page 9

Soldering kit, page 9

Masking tape

FINISHED SIZE
Pendant, 2¾ x 1 inch
(7 x 2.5 cm)

DESIGNER'S NOTE
Wrap the tips of the
round-nose pliers in
masking tape to prevent
marring the metal.

▶ ▶ ▶ **Go**

1. With round-nose pliers, make a 6-mm loop at one end of each wire. Use flat-nose pliers to make a 45-degree bend in the wire at the base of each loop. Use snips to cut the wires, leaving a 1½-inch (3.8 cm) tail on each wire. File each wire end.

2. Using the flat side of a chasing hammer, hammer the wires flat on top of a steel block or anvil.

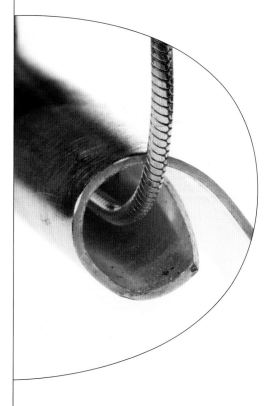

3. Arrange the wires in a pattern on the 20-gauge sterling silver sheet, leaving at least ½ inch (1.3 cm) of empty sheet at the top. Sweat solder the wires in place on the silver sheet. Check to be sure that all wire elements are completely soldered; re-solder any gaps. Snip the ends of the wires flush with the silver sheet.

4. Open the rollers on the rolling mill so that the silver sheet with the attached wires fits snugly in between. Roll the piece through the mill, then anneal. Slightly tighten the rollers and roll the sheet through the mill again, then anneal. Repeat this process until the wires are flush with the surface of the silver sheet.

5. File any sharp metal edges. Using round-nose pliers, bend the top of the sheet to create a bail. Be sure to create a full loop so the pendant will be secure on the chain.

6. Using 600-grit sandpaper, hand sand the pendant in a circular motion to create a brushed surface. Thread the chain through the bail.

▶ ▶ **Get Set**

Yellow gold sheet, 14 karat,
30 gauge, 5.1 x 0.4 cm

Yellow gold round wire,
14 karat, 20 gauge,
2½ inches (6.4 cm)

Cultured pearl, 5 mm

Cultured pearl, 3 mm

Cultured pearl, 2 mm

Round yellow gold snake
chain, 14 karat, 1.2 mm,
20 inches (50.8 cm)

Bench tool kit, page 9

Soldering kit, page 9

FINISHED SIZE
Pendant, 1¼ x ½ inch
(3.2 x 1.3 cm)

▶ ▶ ▶ **Go**

1. Use a jeweler's saw to cut the gold sheet to a 4.4 x 0.4-cm rectangle. With a file, taper the gold rectangle from 4 mm at one end to 2 mm at the other end. Shape the sheet with pliers into a squiggle, such as the extended S shape shown.

2. Drill four holes through the gold squiggle shape from the top to the bottom.

3. Using round-nose pliers, bend the leftover gold sheet to form a U-shaped bail.

4. Apply flux to one end of the 20-gauge round wire and melt the wire with a torch to make a ball.

5. Solder the bail on top of the gold squiggle shape with bail holes facing to the side when the squiggle lies flat.

6. Thread the 20-gauge wire through the top hole of the squiggle, then add the 5-mm pearl. Continue threading the 20-gauge wire through the next hole, and add the 3-mm pearl. Thread the wire through the third hole and add the 2-mm pearl.

7. Thread the 20-gauge wire through the fourth hole and ball the end of the wire at the bottom to complete the construction.

8. Use the flexible shaft with soft buffing attachments and rouge compound to polish the pendant. Thread the snake chain through the bail.

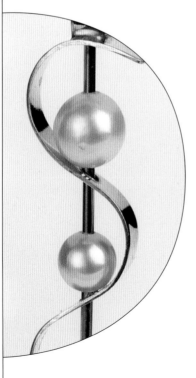

POLISHING • HAMMERING • SAWING • FILING
SANDING • FORMING • DRILLING

▶▶ **Get Set**

Sterling silver sheet,
   21 gauge, ⅞ x 1¼ inches
   (2.2 x 3.2 cm)

Sterling silver earring post
   with 1-mm pad

Half-drilled button pearl,
   8 to 9 mm

Sterling silver snake chain
   with clasp, 16 inches
   (40.6 cm)

Photocopied design
   template ❶

Bench tool kit, page 9

Ball peen hammer

Epoxy

FINISHED SIZE
Pendant, ¾ x 1 inch
(1.9 x 2.5 cm)

▶▶▶ **Go**

1. Polish the silver sheet and place it on a steel block. Hammer the bottom four-fifths of the sheet with the ball end of a ball peen hammer. This will cause the sheet to curve in addition to creating a hammered texture.

2. Protect the front surface of the silver sheet with clear tape.

3. Transfer the photocopied design template of the pear shape onto the silver sheet. Cut out the shape. File, sand, and polish the cut edges.

4. Bend the top one-fifth of the silver shape forward and under with round-nose pliers, forming a tube that will act as a bail. Make sure the point of the bail touches the back of the sheet so the bail secures the chain to the pendant. Sand and polish the metal to remove any scratches.

5. Following the design template, mark and drill the hole for the pearl peg.

6. With the pad at the back of the pendant, insert the earring post through the drilled hole. Cut the post wire to length so it goes halfway into the pearl. (If necessary, drill the hole deeper in the pearl with a standard bit.) With a file or saw blade, rough up the surface of the post so the epoxy will adhere better.

7. Place a piece of tape on the back of the pendant to hold the post in place and epoxy the pearl onto the post. When the epoxy is dry, remove the tape and thread the chain through the bail.

❶

▶▶ ▶ Get Set

Fine silver round wire,
24 gauge, 60 inches
(1.5 m)

Sterling silver flat curb
chain with clasp,
1.5 mm, 16 inches
(40.6 cm)

Soldering kit, page 9

FINISHED SIZE
Necklace, 16 inches
(40.6 cm); pendant,
2¼ x ½ inch (5.7 x 1.3 cm)

▶▶ ▶ Go

1. Cut 41 pieces of the 24-gauge fine silver wire, each 1¼ inches (3.2 cm) long. Use a torch to melt a ball on one end of each wire.

2. Mark the center of the flat curb chain. Suspend the chain between two sets of cross-locking tweezers, using a third hand if necessary.

4. Beginning at the marked center point, thread a balled wire through each link of the chain. Place an equal number of wires on either side of the center link and one wire through the center link.

5. Working on one wire at a time, use a torch to ball the opposite end. Use a solder pick to hold the other wires out of the way of the flame.

6. If needed, remove torch soot from the wires and chain links by very quickly dipping them in hot pickle. Important: Do not pickle the clasp, as the steel spring will contaminate your pickle. Rinse and dry the necklace.

Want to Make
Another Necklace?

This design is very adaptable. You can use copper wire instead of fine silver, add more or use fewer decorative wires, make the wires shorter or longer, or vary their length. Consider the possibilities!

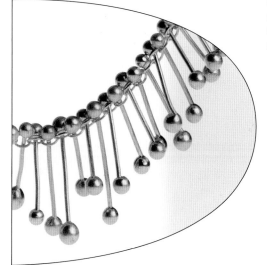

▶▶ ▶ Get Set

Sterling silver round wire, 24 gauge, 5 feet (1.5 m)

36 sterling silver donut beads, each 3 x 2 mm, 1-mm hole

2 soldered sterling silver jump rings, 20 gauge, each 3 mm

4 sterling silver jump rings, 20 gauge, each 3 mm

Sterling silver curb chain, 5 mm, 1 inch (2.5 cm)

Sterling silver lobster clasp, 10 mm

Bench tool kit, page 9

Soldering kit, page 9

Tumbler with steel shot

FINISHED SIZE
Necklace, 17 to 18 inches (43.2 to 45.7 cm)

DESIGNER'S NOTE
Depending on the size of the balls melted on the ends of the wires, your chain may end up longer or shorter. Add extra links if you wish to extend the length of your chain.

▶▶▶ Go

1. Cut the 24-gauge wire into 35 pieces, each 1¼ inches (3.2 cm) long. In bundles of 10, slightly bend the middle of the wires with your fingers to create very wide U shapes. Cut two 1½-inch (4 cm) lengths of the 24-gauge wire and bend these in the same manner.

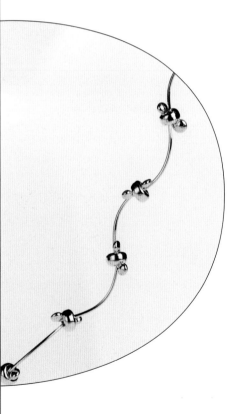

2. Arrange the torch so you do not need to hold it. Melt a ball on one end of each wire length, making each ball about 2 mm in diameter. Melt a larger ball on one end of the 4-cm pieces. Let the wires air cool.

3. Thread two beads onto 18 of the shorter wires. Ball the other ends of these wires, making sure the balls on both ends are large enough to secure the beads. The finished length of these links should be ⅝ inch (1.5 cm). Let the wires air cool.

4. Thread one of the open wire lengths through two adjacent beads, each from a closed link. Use a torch to ball the end of the open wire. Each bead should have a metal ball on each side.

5. Continue joining the links and melting the ends until all the wires are joined and you have reached the desired length for your chain.

6. Thread one soldered jump ring onto one of the 4-cm wire lengths. The balled end of this wire should be large enough to secure the jump ring. Thread the open end of this length through the bead at one end of the chain. Melt a ball on the open end. Repeat for other end of the chain.

7. Connect the curb chain to the handmade chain with a jump ring. Solder the jump ring closed. Attach the clasp with the remaining jump ring. Solder the jump ring closed, keeping the heat away from the clasp to protect the mechanism.

8. Polish the necklace in a tumbler with steel shot until shiny.

▶ ▶ Get Set

Fine silver wire, 14 gauge,
24 inches (61 cm)

Sterling silver jump ring,
16 gauge, 7 mm

Leather cord, 1 mm,
26 inches (66 cm)

2 sterling silver crimp
tubes, each 3 mm

Sterling silver clasp

Bench tool kit, page 9

Soldering kit, page 9

FINISHED SIZE
Pendant, 1½ x 3½ inches
(3.8 x 8.9 cm)

▶ ▶ ▶ Go

1. Wrap the 16-gauge wire around a 15-mm mandrel to make five jump rings. Wrap the 16-gauge wire around an 18-mm mandrel to make two jump rings. Saw the jump rings apart, and close the jump rings with your fingers.

2. Use a torch to fuse the joints of the seven jump rings.

3. One at a time, place each jump ring on a ring mandrel and hammer it with the flat side of a chasing hammer.

4. Following design template ❶, position the fused rings in a pattern on a soldering block. Solder the rings together at each joint.

5. Rub the pendant with a brass brush to polish it. Attach the pendant to the leather cord with the jump ring.

6. Attach the clasp by threading each end of the leather cord through a crimp bead and a side of the clasp and then back through the crimp bead. Use crimping pliers to secure each crimp bead on the leather cord. Trim the tails of the cord with snips.

Want to Make Another Necklace?

Experiment with a variety of jump ring sizes to achieve different looks.

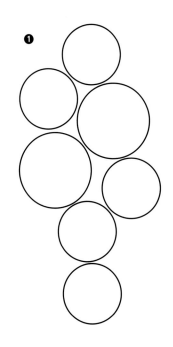

❶

DESIGNER: **ERICA STANKWYTCH BAILEY**

**USING A DISK CUTTER • FILING • FUSING • DRILLING
WIREWORK • ADDING A PATINA**

▶▶ Get Set

Sterling silver sheet,
  20 gauge, 5.1 x 5.1 cm

Sterling silver sheet,
  24 gauge, 5.1 x 5.1 cm

2 sterling silver jump rings,
  18 gauge, 3.2 mm in
  diameter

Sterling silver chain, cable,
  or cord, 16 inches
  (40.6 cm)

Bench tool kit, page 9

Soldering kit, page 9

Disk cutter, with 4.1 cm,
  1.6 cm, and 6.4 mm
  disk-cutting capacity

Liver of sulfur

Steel wool, super fine

FINISHED SIZE
Pendant, 4.1 cm in
diameter

▶▶▶ Go

1. Using the 4.1-cm disk cutter, cut one disk from the 20-gauge sterling silver sheet. This will be referred to as the "large disk."

2. Using the 1.6-cm disk cutter, cut a disk out of the interior of the large disk. This interior disk can be centered or it can be off-center as shown in the project. (The 1.6-cm silver disk cut out of the large disk is not used in this project. Use it for other creative purposes.)

3. Using the 6.4-mm disk cutter, cut 11 small disks from the 24-gauge sterling silver sheet. These will be referred to as the "small disks."

4. File the edges of the large disk and the small disks smooth.

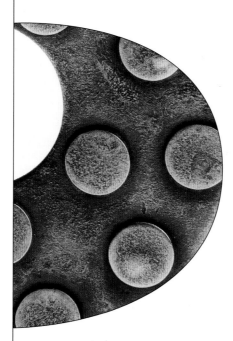

5. Place the large disk on a soldering block and coat in a thin layer of flux. Arrange the small disks on the surface of the large disk in an interesting pattern. (In this project, the disks are evenly spaced with some positioned close to the edges.) Allow the flux to dry.

6. Heat the entire piece, slowly moving the torch over the piece and using the part of the flame just past the blue cone. The surface will begin to look fluid, like mercury. It is at this point that fusing occurs. Lightly fuse the metal to simply connect the pieces, or fuse it a bit longer to create a surface texture similar to reticulation. Pickle, rinse, and dry the piece.

7. Confirm that all small disks are fully fused. If not, repeat steps 5 and 6.

8. Decide how you want the pendant to hang and determine where to drill the holes for the bail. Near the top edge of the pendant, center punch two divots approximately 3 mm apart. Drill two holes using a 1.6-mm bit. Remove any burrs with a file. Thread one 3.2-mm jump ring through each drilled hole, and fully close the jump rings. (Soldering the jump rings closed would be advantageous but is not necessary.)

9. Submerge the pendant and the chain or cable in a liver of sulfur solution until the pieces turn black/charcoal grey. (The time of the bath is determined by the strength and age of the solution.) Remove the metal, rinse thoroughly, and dry completely. Thread the chain through the two jump rings.

10. Gently rub the pendant with steel wool to remove the dark patina from the high points and emphasize the texture and pattern created by fusing.

DESIGNER: **NINA DINOFF**

DRILLING • BALLING WIRE • WIREWORK • SOLDERING • POLISHING

▶▶ Get Set

48 sterling silver disks,
    each ¼ inch (6 mm) in
    diameter

20 sterling silver disks,
    each ½ inch (1.3 cm) in
    diameter

Fine silver wire, 22 gauge,
    24 inches (61 cm)

Sterling silver flat cable
    chain, 2.5 mm, 15½
    inches (39.4 cm)

Sterling silver spring ring
    clasp

Sterling silver jump ring,
    20 gauge, 3 mm

Sterling silver jump ring,
    20 gauge, 5 mm

Bench tool kit, page 9

Torch

Tweezers

Tumbler with stainless
    steel shot

FINISHED SIZE
Chain, 15½ inches (39.4 cm)

DESIGNER'S NOTE
After balling the wire ends
and before adding more
silver disks, make sure to
quench the necklace in water
so you don't burn yourself.

TIME SAVER
It is possible to thread
several silver disks onto
the chain and then add the
second disks before melting
balls on the open wires ends.

▶▶▶ Go

1. Use a center punch to mark the center of each silver disk. Using tweezers to firmly hold each disk in place, drill each center-punched disk.

2. Cut 34 pieces of 22-gauge wire, each ½ inch (1.3 cm) long. Use a torch to ball one end of each wire.

3. Thread a length of balled wire through 24 of the ¼-inch (6 mm) disks and 10 of the ½-inch (1.3 cm) disks.

4. Thread the wire of a ¼-inch (6 mm) disk through the sterling silver flat cable chain, ⅝ inch (1.6 cm) from the end. Thread a drilled ¼-inch (6 mm) disk onto the wire, and use snips to trim the remaining wire to 3 mm. Use a torch to ball the wire end to secure

the disks. Following the pattern in the project photo, repeat this process with the remaining large and small silver disks, spacing each set of discs ⅜ inch (9.5 mm) apart.

5. Attach the clasp to one end of the chain with the 3-mm jump ring. Attach the 5-mm jump ring to the opposite end of the chain. Solder the jump rings closed.

6. Pickle the necklace, then polish it in a tumbler with stainless steel shot.

Want to Make Another Necklace?

This inspired design lends itself to lots of looks. Oxidizing the necklace with a liver-of-sulfur patina, using metals with contrasting colors, connecting the disks with drilled wires instead of chain (see variation), and attaching stone beads to the wire ends are just a few of your options.

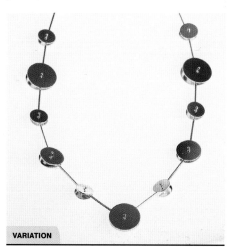

VARIATION

Get Ready

SAWING • SANDING • DRILLING • DAPPING • WIREWORK • SOLDERING
BALLING WIRE • FINISHING • GLUING • RIVETING

▶▶ Get Set

5 white table-tennis balls

10 brass disks, 24 gauge,
 2.5 cm in diameter

5 round pearls, drilled,
 7 mm

Black buna cord, 6 mm,
 18 inches (45.7 cm)

2 silver round wires,
 18 gauge, each 3.2 cm

2 silver tubes, 7.8 mm OD,
 7.3 mm ID, each 1.6 cm

Commercial clasp,
 S hook or standard
 hook with jump ring

5 silver round wires,
 18 gauge, each 2.5 cm

5 pieces 14-karat yellow
 gold, 28 gauge, each
 1.3 cm square

2 silver round wires,
 18 gauge, each 1.6 cm

5 black rubber O-rings,
 5-mm diameter hole

Bench tool kit, page 9

Soldering kit, page 9

Masking tape

Sandpaper, 220 grit

Brass brush

Cyanoacrylate glue or
 5-minute epoxy

Small brush for applying
 adhesive

FINISHED SIZE
18 inches (45.7 cm),
pendants from 2.5 to 5 cm

▶▶▶ Go

1. Before sawing the table tennis balls, wrap a length of masking tape around each one to use as a measuring and cutting guide. Leaving part of the sticky side of the tape exposed will help you handle the balls. Using a jeweler's saw, cut two balls slightly larger than one-half of the diameter, cut two balls one-quarter of the diameter, and cut one ball three-quarters of the diameter. Remove the masking tape and sand the cut edges smooth with 220-grit sandpaper. Drill the center of the bottom of each ball with a 1.5-mm bit.

2. Use a dapping block and punches to dome the brass disks to fit the curvature of the table-tennis balls. Drill the bottom centers of the brass domes using a 1.5-mm bit.

3. Using a 1.5-mm bit, enlarge the pearl holes by drilling them half of the way through on each side. Alternate dipping the bit in water and drilling. Allow the pearls to air dry.

4. Measure and mark these points from one end of the buna cord: 17.1 cm, 19.7 cm, 22.9 cm, 26 cm, and 28.6 cm. Using a 1.5-mm bit, drill through the cord at a slight angle at the marked points.

5. Use round-nose pliers to curve the two 3.2-cm pieces of 18-gauge silver wire into U shapes. Fit 4 mm of the formed wire ends inside of the silver tubing. Solder the ends of the bent wire into the tubes with easy solder. If you're using a clasp with a jump ring, be sure to thread it onto one of the U shapes before soldering it.

6. Use a torch to ball the ends of the five 2.5-cm wire lengths. Melt the small pieces of 14-karat gold into tiny balls on a soldering surface.

7. Brush all metal parts with a brass brush for a shiny finish.

8. Gently push a balled silver wire into each of the drilled holes in the buna cord, so the balled end rests against the cord. Assemble each blossom, so the largest table-tennis ball is in the center and the smallest balls are at the ends. On each balled wire, thread a brass disk, the table-tennis ball, and another brass disk. Use snips to cut the remaining wire ends to 3 mm. Apply cyanoacrylate glue to the trimmed ends, and set the pearls. Let the glue dry.

9. Fit an O-ring over each pearl, using the natural tension of the rubber to keep the ring in place. Use the cyanoacrylate glue to secure a tiny gold sphere to each pearl.

10. Fit the buna cord all the way into the finished end caps. Using the 1.5-mm bit, drill a straight hole through the end cap and the cord 5 mm from the bottom of the end cap. Insert a 1.6-cm wire through each drilled hole. Trim and rivet the wires.

▶ ▶ Get Set

Rectangular silver wire,
6 x 1.65 mm, 5 cm long

Illusion film or 0.4-mm-thick
polypropylene sheet,
14 strips, each 9 x 1 cm

16 earring posts with
5-mm cups

Illusion film or 0.4-mm-thick
polypropylene sheet,
2 strips, each 11 x 1 cm

Silver sheet, 18 gauge,
1.5 cm square

Silver sheet, 24 gauge,
1 cm square

Bench tool kit, page 9

Soldering kit, page 9

DESIGNER'S NOTE

Illusion film is a multilensed
polycarbonate. Thousands
of minute parabolic lenses
are molded into the surface
on both sides of the film.
These lenses create a
pattern of absorption and
reflection of light, resulting in
unique optical effects.

▶ ▶ ▶ Go

1. Measure and cut three 1.5-cm lengths of the rectangular wire. Set the dividers at 1.5 mm. Use the edges of the metal to draw an interior rectangle on each silver piece. Drill a hole inside the interior rectangle, and pierce and saw out the form on each piece. You now have three small silver "frames."

2. Anneal the 18-gauge sterling silver square, and quench and pickle the metal. Place the silver square facedown on a soldering block. Position one long side of a silver frame near one edge of the silver square. (Most of the frame should hang off the square.) Solder the frame to the square with hard solder. Quench and pickle the metal.

3. Mark a centerline on the 24-gauge silver square. Using flat pliers, bend the metal into a U shape along the marked line. (This is the hook for the clasp.)

4. Place the 18-gauge silver square facedown on a soldering block. Position the bend of the silver hook near the edge of the square, across from the silver frame. Solder the hook in place with medium solder. Quench and pickle the metal.

5. Mark and drill two holes on two of the short plastic strips, each 5 mm in from an end.

6. Mark and drill three holes on each of the remaining short plastic strips. The locations for the holes are: 5 mm in from one end; 5 mm in from the other end; and 3.5 cm in from one end.

7. Mark and drill four holes on each of the long plastic strips. The locations for the holes are: 3 mm in from one end; 3 mm in from the other end; 2.2 cm in from one end; and 3.5 cm in from the other end. Divide all the drilled plastic strips into two equal piles.

8. Feed a short plastic strip with two holes through a silver frame. Push an earring post through the two holes and through the middle one on one of the three-hole strips. Bend the very end of the earring post with round pliers, forming a small loop. (The plastic material should be able to move quite freely.)

9. Attach five more three-hole plastic strips in this fashion, feeding a post through the two end holes and then through the middle hole on the next strip and looping the post to secure. Feed the next post through the two end holes and then through the furthest hole in on a four-hole strip. Loop the post. Feed the longer end of the strip through the hole in the silver clasp. Bend the end of the strip back, overlapping the other end. Push an earring post through the three holes, this time positioning the cup on the outside of the strip. Loop the post.

10. Repeat step 9 to construct the second side of the necklace, starting the first link in the same silver frame and working in the opposite direction. (The earring cups will all be on the inside of the necklace.) Instead of feeding the final four-hole strip though the clasp, feed it through the third silver frame.

DESIGNER: **DILYANA EVTIMOVA**

DESIGNER: **DANIELLE LAUREN SMITH**

SAWING • **DRILLING** • **DAPPING** • **SANDING** • **RIVETING** • **FILING**
SOLDERING (OPTIONAL) • **USING A DISK CUTTER (OPTIONAL)**

▶ ▶ Get Set

Sterling silver sheet,
18 gauge, 1 x 1 inch
(2.5 x 2.5 cm)

Sterling silver jump ring,
20 gauge, 4 mm

Sterling silver oval link
chain, 4 mm, 25 inches
(63.5 cm)

Craft foam sheet

Sterling silver tubing, 2 mm
OD, 1.3 mm ID

Sterling silver wire, 16
gauge, 1 inch (2.5 cm)

Bench tool kit, page 9

Soldering kit, page 9
(optional)

Disk cutter or circle punch,
¾ inch (1.9 cm) and
⅝ inch (1.6 cm)

Ball burr, 1.5 mm

Hole punch

FINISHED SIZE
Pendant, 1¼ x 1¼ x ¼ inch
(3.2 x 3.2 x 0.6 cm)

▶ ▶ ▶ Go

1. Use a saw or a disk cutter to cut two disks from the 18-gauge silver sheet, each ½ inch (1.3 cm) in diameter. Mark and drill a 1-mm hole in the center of each disk.

2. Dome each silver disk with a dapping block and punch. Use a 1.5-mm ball burr to countersink the hole on the top of each dome. Sand domes to desired finish using 220-grit sandpaper.

3. Link the 4-mm, 20-gauge jump ring through each end of the silver chain. Solder the jump ring closed (optional).

4. Use a disk cutter or a circle punch to cut eight foam disks—four that are ¾ inch (1.9 cm) in diameter and four that are ⅝ inch (1.6 cm) in diameter. Use the hole punch to cut a hole in each foam circle, 2 mm inside the edge.

5. Use a saw to cut a piece of silver tubing that is 9 mm long. Use a saw to cut a piece of 16-gauge wire that is 13 mm long.

6. Thread the silver tube through the four large foam disks, two small foam disks, the jump ring attached to the chain, and two more small foam discs. Thread the wire through the 9-mm tube. Add one domed cap to each end of the wire.

7. Rivet the wire using a chasing hammer and a steel block and taking care to not get the foam dirty. File and sand the rivets flush.

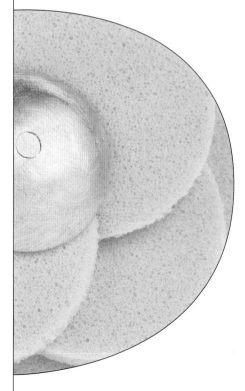

DESIGNER: **ANN L. LUMSDEN**

▶ ▶ Get Set

Sterling silver sheet,
24 gauge, 1½ x 2 inches
(3.8 x 5.1 cm)

Heavyweight paper

2 paper punches, butterfly
shapes

4 sterling silver jump rings,
20 gauge, each 4 mm

Amethyst briolette,
1 x 10 mm

Sterling silver round wire,
24 gauge, 1 inch
(2.5 cm)

Sterling silver figaro chain
with clasp, 2 mm,
16 inches (40.6 cm)

Bench tool kit, page 9

Rolling mill

Clear tape

Marking pen

FINISHED SIZE
Pendant, 1¼ x 2 inches
(3.2 x 5.1 cm)

▶ ▶ ▶ Go

1. Anneal and polish the silver sheet.

2. Cut a piece of heavyweight paper that is larger than the silver sheet. Punch out the two butterfly shapes, leaving at least 8 mm between the two designs.

3. Center the punched paper on the polished front surface of the silver sheet. Place a plain piece of the same paper on the back surface, sandwiching the silver sheet between the two pieces of paper. Adjust the

rollers of the rolling mill slightly thinner than the "sandwich." Roll the paper and metal through the rolling mill.

4. Protect the front surface of the printed silver sheet with clear tape. If necessary, flatten the sheet by hand or with flat-nose pliers that have cushioned surfaces.

5. Use a marker to draw a line around the raised butterflies, 3 to 4 mm outside the edge of the design. Saw out the marked shapes, then file, sand, and polish the edges.

6. Use a scribe to mark the location of the jump rings (in the four corners of the large butterfly, and the two upper corners of the small butterfly) and the amethyst briolette (in the bottom center of the small butterfly). Drill holes at the marked points.

7. Insert the 24-gauge silver wire through the hole in the amethyst briolette, form a loop with round-nose pliers, and attach the stone to the bottom of the butterfly. Attach the two butterflies with two 4-mm jump rings.

8. Snip the chain in half. Attach the ends of the chain to the top silver butterfly with two 4-mm jump rings.

**SAWING • ANNEALING • FORMING • FILING • SANDING
WIREWORK • SOLDERING • DRILLING • BALLING WIRE**

▶ ▶ **Get Set**

Sterling silver sheet,
   22 gauge, ½ x 1½ inches
   (1.3 x 3.8 cm)

Sterling silver wire, 18
   gauge, ½ inch (1.3 cm)

Sterling silver wire, 20
   gauge, 1½ inches
   (3.8 cm)

Fluorite bead, 7 mm square

Sterling silver chain,
   16 inches (40.6 cm)

Bench tool kit, page 9

Soldering kit, page 9

Sinusoidal stake

FINISHED SIZE
Pendant, ½ x 1½ inches
(1.3 x 3.8 cm)

DESIGNER'S NOTE
This is an excellent project
for scrap sterling silver
sheet, as the size of the
pendant can vary. Leftover
roller-printed stock and
remainders from etched
sheets can add interesting
texture to this pendant.

▶ ▶ ▶ **Go**

1. Anneal the ½ x 1½-inch (1.3 x 3.8 cm)
piece of sterling silver sheet.

2. Form the sterling silver sheet into the
shape of a potato chip by bending the metal
in the crook of a sinusoidal stake with a
rawhide hammer.

VARIATION

3. File the edges of the formed silver sheet
smooth. Sand any tool marks. If using
textured scrap metal, make sure any roller
printing or etched designs remain intact.

4. Using round-nose pliers, form the
18-gauge round wire into a U shape for the
bail. File and sand the wire ends flat.

5. Solder the bail to the back of the pendant,
about ³⁄₁₆ inch (5 mm) from the top edge
and centered.

6. Measure and mark a centered point that
is ½ inch (1.3 cm) from the bottom edge of
the pendant. Drill a 0.8-mm hole in the metal
at the marked point.

7. Use a torch to ball one end of the
1½-inch (3.8 cm) 20-gauge wire. Thread the
wire through the bead and the silver sheet
from the front. Using chain-nose pliers, coil
the wire and then bend the coil so it rests flat
against the back of the pendant. Thread a
chain through the bail.

WIREWORK • **FILING** • **SANDING** • **SOLDERING** • **SAWING**
ROLLER PRINTING • **BALLING WIRE** • **POLISHING**

▶ ▶ Get Set

Sterling silver round wire, 16 gauge, 6¾ inches (15.9 cm)

6 sterling silver jump rings, 18 gauge, each 5 mm

Sterling silver sheet, 22 gauge, ¾ x ¾ inch (1.9 x 1.9 cm)

Small piece of lace

Sterling silver box chain, 1 mm, 17 inches (43.2 cm)

Sterling silver round wire, 18 gauge, 2½ inches (6.4 cm)

Photocopied design template ❶

Bench tool kit, page 9

Soldering kit, page 9

Bracelet mandrel or similar curved surface

Double-sided tape

Planishing hammer

Rolling mill

Tumbler with stainless steel shot

FINISHED SIZE
Necklace, 20 inches (50.8 cm); pendant, 2½ x ½ inch (6.4 x 1.3 cm)

▶ ▶ ▶ Go

1. Use snips to cut three pieces of 16-gauge sterling silver round wire: two 2¼ inches (5.7 cm) and one 1¾ inches (4.4 cm). Use your fingers and a rawhide mallet to bend the wire over a bracelet mandrel to match the project design. File and sand the wire ends.

2. Arrange the wires on a soldering block. Solder the wires together at the joints. Solder a jump ring to each top corner of the bent wire piece.

3. With a planishing hammer, slightly flatten the soldered wire piece.

4. Using double-sided tape, attach the photocopied tree template to the sterling silver sheet. Pierce and saw out the design.

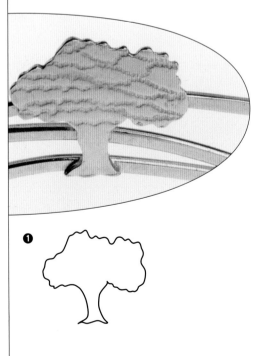

❶

5. Texture the boughs of the silver tree by roller printing it with a piece of lace. File and sand the textured silver tree.

6. Solder the silver tree to the wire piece.

7. Use snips to cut the chain into two 8½-inch (21.6 cm) lengths. Solder an open jump ring to each chain end. Join the jump ring at one end of each chain section to one jump ring on each side of the pendant.

8. Use round-nose pliers to form an S clasp from the 18-gauge sterling silver wire. Ball the ends of the wire and solder one side of the S together. Flatten the S clasp with a planishing hammer. Attach the clasp to one jump ring at the end of the chain.

9. Solder all jump rings closed. Note: Be careful when soldering jump rings to a box or snake chain—the solder will run along the length of the chain very quickly. Use easy solder and aim the heat toward the jump ring and away from the chain.

10. Polish the necklace in a tumbler with stainless steel shot.

Want to Make Another Necklace?

With this basic design as a foundation, there's lots of room to let your imagination run wild. For instance, a gold or copper tree would look fantastic, as would stringing the pendant on a natural cord or a length of beads.

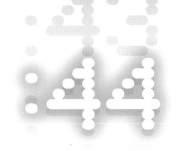

→ Get Ready

SAWING • **ROLLER PRINTING** • **FILING** • **SOLDERING**
FINISHING • **KNOTTING LEATHER**

▶▶ Get Set

Fine silver sheet, 18 gauge,
   1½ x 2 inches
   (3.8 x 5.1 cm)

Brass round wire,
   12 gauge, 12 inches
   (30.5 cm)

2 sterling silver jump rings,
   18 gauge, each 6 mm

Round leather cord, 2 mm,
   50 inches (1.3 m)

Photocopied design
   template ❶

Bench tool kit, page 9

Soldering kit, page 9

Epoxy

FINISHED SIZE
Pendant, 1¼ x 2 inches
(3.2 x 5.1 cm)

DESIGNER'S NOTE
Roller printing loose wires
is not an exact science, so
your design will most likely
come out differently than the
one pictured. Experiment
with roller printing a variety
of wire shapes.

▶▶▶ Go

1. Attach the photocopied design template to the fine silver sheet and saw out the shape. Remove the template and anneal the fine silver sheet.

2. Bend the 12-gauge brass wire into freeform circles and shapes.

3. Position the brass wires on the fine silver sheet. Place a piece of scrap metal on top of the wires, forming a "sandwich."

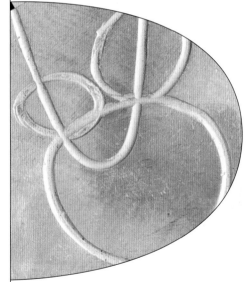

4. Adjust the rollers on the rolling mill so the metal "sandwich" fits snugly in between, and then move the rollers a tiny bit closer together. Roll the sandwich through the rolling mill.

5. Use a file to make the edges of the pendant straight and smooth.

6. Solder the two jump rings on edge to the back of the pendant, above the centerline and approximately ½ inch (1.3 cm) apart. Use 400-grit sandpaper to give the pendant a final finish.

7. Thread the leather cord through both jump rings on the back of the pendant. Overlap the ends of the cord. Using 1 inch (2.5 cm) of leather cord, tie an overhand knot around the opposite cord end. Trim the leather cord tail with snips. Repeat with the leather cord on the other end. Slide the knots back and forth to vary the necklace length, and adjust the knot tension accordingly. Secure the knots with epoxy and let dry.

❶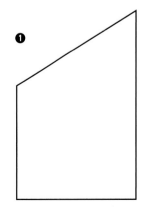

USING A DISK CUTTER • HAMMERING • DRILLING • SANDING • WIREWORK
SOLDERING • POLISHING • ADDING A PATINA (OPTIONAL)

▶▶ Get Set

Sterling silver sheet,
24 gauge, 1 x 8 inches
(2.5 x 20.3 cm)

16 sterling silver jump
rings, 20 gauge, each
4 mm

Sterling silver flat draw
cable chain, 2.6 mm,
36 inches (91.4 cm)

Bench tool kit, page 9

Soldering kit, page 9

Riveting hammer

Liver of sulfur, optional

FINISHED SIZE
Necklace, 42 inches;
pendants from ⅝ inch
(1.6 cm) to 1 inch (2.5 cm)

▶▶▶ Go

1. Use the disk cutter to cut two 1-inch
(2.5 cm) disks, three ¾-inch (1.9 cm) disks,
and three ½-inch (1.3 cm) disks from the
24-gauge sterling silver sheet.

2. Hammer the silver disks on a steel block
with the peen side of a riveting hammer to
add texture in a radial pattern. Leave the
warpage created by the hammering.

3. Mark and drill two 1-mm holes on the
metal disks, on opposite sides and 2 mm in
from the edge. Sand each disk smooth.

4. Use snips to cut the chain into eight
pieces, either all the same length or
various lengths.

5. Use flat-nose and chain-nose pliers to
connect a jump ring and section of chain
to each disk, making a chain with no clasp.
Solder each jump ring closed. Polish the
necklace with a brass brush.

Have Time to Spare?

Add a patina to the finished necklace or
create a second one from a different color
of metal.

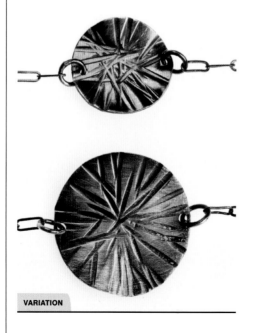

VARIATION

**SAWING • FILING • SOLDERING • DAPPING
HAMMERING • ADDING A PATINA**

▶▶ **Get Set**

Sterling silver round bead
    wire, 8 gauge, 3 inches
    (7.6 cm)

Sterling silver disk,
    24 gauge, ½ inch
    (1.3 cm) in diameter

Sterling silver fine twist
    chain with clasp,
    20 inches (50.8 cm)

Design template ❶

Bench tool kit, page 9

Soldering kit, page 9

Liver of sulfur

Steel wool

FINISHED SIZE
Pendant, 1⅛ inches
(2.8 cm) in diameter

▶▶▶ **Go**

1. Use a jeweler's saw to cut a 3-inch (7.6 cm) piece of 8-gauge round bead wire. File the ends flat.

2. Without worrying about the shape of the wire, use your fingers and flat-nose pliers to bend the round bead wire so the ends fit together. Solder the joint.

3. Using design template ❶ as a guide, saw the flower shape from the ½-inch (1.3 cm) silver disk. File the edges of the flower smooth.

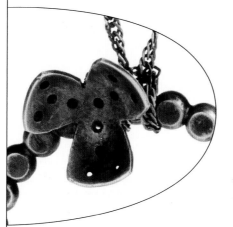

4. Using a hammer and center punch, randomly indent dots on the silver flower. Place the flower in a dapping block with the dots facing up. Use a punch to slightly dome the flower.

5. With your fingers and then a hammer, form the bead wire into a circle on a ring mandrel. Place the wire circle on a steel block and hammer it with the flat face of a chasing hammer to flatten the beads.

6. Place the domed silver flower upside down on a soldering block. Use a third hand to hold the wire circle on the center of the flower. Solder the wire circle to the flower.

7. Slip the closed chain through the center of the pendant. Bring the clasp over the bead wire and through the loop in the chain to secure the pendant to the chain.

8. Patina the necklace with a liver-of-sulfur solution. Lightly brush the necklace with steel wool.

❶

▶ ▶ Get Set

Sterling silver wire,
   6 gauge, 16 inches
   (40.6 cm)

14 sterling silver jump
   rings, 12 gauge, each
   7 mm

6 sterling silver jump rings,
   14 gauge, each 8 mm

Sterling silver wire,
   14 gauge, 2 inches
   (5.1 cm)

Bench tool kit, page 9

Soldering kit, page 9

Liver of sulfur

Steel wool, fine

FINISHED SIZE
18 inches (45.7 cm)

▶ ▶ ▶ Go

1. Use your fingers to bend the 6-gauge wire into a circle that is 4½ inches (11.4 cm) in diameter.

2. Use a jeweler's saw to cut the silver circle into seven sections: six measuring 2 inches (5.1 cm) and one measuring 4 inches (10.2 cm). File and sand the edges flat.

3. File each 7-mm jump ring flat on the outside edge at the joint. Solder the flattened edge of one jump ring to each end of each wire section, horizontal to the curve of the wire.

4. Use the 8-mm jump rings to connect the curved wire sections, making sure the 4-inch (10.2 cm) section is in the center of the necklace.

5. Using round-nose pliers, form a simple S clasp with the 14-gauge wire. Attach the clasp to a jump ring at one the end of the necklace. Solder the S clasp closed and ball the ends of the wire.

6. Sand all solder joints smooth, making sure to sand off any firescale. Apply a liver-of-sulfur solution to the necklace. To give the necklace a final finish, rub it with fine steel wool to remove the patina from most of the necklace except the joints.

Want to Make Another Necklace?

This design also looks great as a short choker. To achieve this, simply remove one link from the chain.

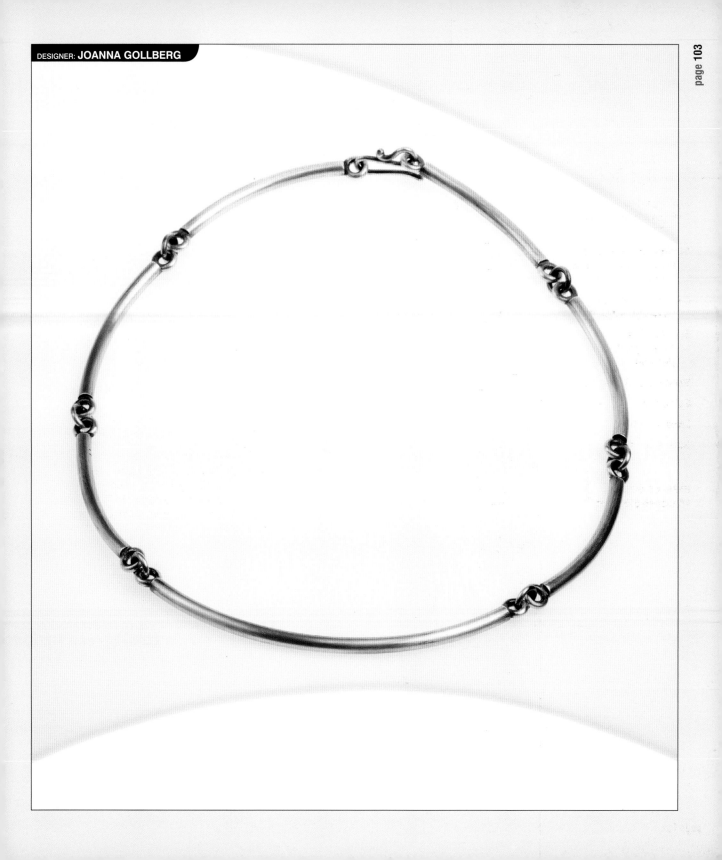

→ Get Ready

SAWING · FILING · SANDING · SOLDERING · ADDING A PATINA

⟶ ►► Get Set

Sterling silver sheet,
26 gauge, 2 x 2 inches
(5.1 x 5.1 cm)

Sterling silver jump ring,
20 gauge, 1.5 mm

Sterling silver cable chain,
1 mm, 16 inches
(40.6 cm)

Wallpaper, any kind,
2 x 2 inches
(5.1 x 5.1 cm)

Photocopied design
templates ❶ and ❷

Bench tool kit, page 9

Soldering kit, page 9

Liver of sulfur

FINISHED SIZE
Pendant, 2¼ x 1⅛ inches
(5.7 cm x 2.9 cm)

→ ►►► Go

1. Transfer the photocopied design template ❶ onto the sheet metal. Make sure to conserve the metal by placing the template on the diagonal on the silver sheet. Saw out the design, then file and sand the edges.

2. Use your fingers to sand the pendant in a circular motion with 400-grit sandpaper.

3. Use wire cutters to snip both ends of the jump ring to form a C shape. File each end flat.

4. Solder the jump ring vertically to the back of the pendant, near the top edge.

5. Apply a liver-of-sulfur solution to the silver pendant and chain. Brush the front and back surfaces of the pendant with a soapy brass brush.

6. Use the photocopied design template ❷ to cut the wallpaper to fit inside the pendant. Place the wallpaper on the metal, and carefully bend the tabs around the wallpaper with flat-nosed pliers.

7. Place the pendant on a steel block and gently tap the tabs down with a wooden mallet. Thread the chain through the bail.

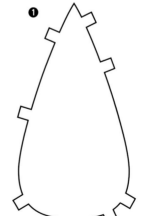

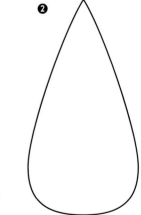

❶   ❷

SAWING • PIERCING • FILING • SANDING • HAMMERING SOLDERING • HAND SEWING • RIVETING • GLUING

▶▶ ▶ Get Set

Sterling silver sheet,
    20 gauge, 3 x 1½ inches
    (7.6 x 3.8 cm)

Sterling silver tube,
    3.25 mm OD, ¼ inch
    (6 mm)

Navy tulle, 5 x 54 inches
    (12.7 x 137.2 cm)

Navy thread, 1 spool

12 to 15 freshwater pearls,
    4 mm

2 sterling silver jump rings,
    16 gauge, each ½ inch
    (1.3 cm)

Sterling silver mesh chain,
    16 or 18 inches
    (40.6 or 45.7 cm)

Photocopied design
    templates ❶ and ❷

Bench tool kit, page 9

Soldering kit, page 9

Double-sided tape

Fabric scissors

Ball-peen hammer

Brass brush

Sewing needle

Glue

Toothpick

FINISHED SIZE
Pendant, 5 x 5 x 1 inch
(12.7 x 12.7 x 2.5 cm)

▶▶ ▶ Go

1. Attach the templates to the silver sheet with double-sided tape. Saw out the decorative shape and the washer shape. Remove the paper and tape from the silver sheet and file or sand the edges of each shape.

2. Place the silver shapes on a steel block and texture them with a ball-peen hammer. With a rawhide mallet, hammer the opposite side of the shapes to flatten them.

3. Use the washer to determine where to place the tube on the back of the decorative silver shape, making sure the washer does not show from the front. Mark this spot with a scribe, and solder the tube in place.

4. Pickle, rinse, and clean all metal parts with a brass brush.

5. Fold the tulle in half lengthwise. Using needle and thread, gather the tulle with a basic running stitch about 5 mm from one long edge. Finish with a tight stitch and knot the thread.

6. Carefully place the tubing in the middle of the tulle. Thread the washer on the tubing and rivet.

7. Trim the tulle with scissors so the bottom section is longer than the top section.

8. Using a small amount of glue on the end of a toothpick, randomly adhere the fresh water pearls to the tulle.

9. Thread the jump rings through the hole on the larger metal shape. Run the chain through the jump rings.

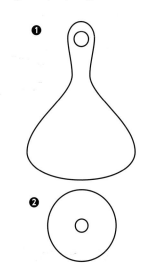

→ Get Ready

MELTING METAL · **SOLDERING** · **FINISHING**
BEZEL SETTING · **WIREWORK**

→ → Get Set

Fine silver scrap or grain

Pre-made sterling silver or
fine silver round bezel,
6 mm

2 sterling silver jump rings,
20 gauge, each 4 mm

Sterling silver ball chain
with clasp, 1.5 mm,
16 inches (40.6 cm)

Round faceted garnet,
6 mm

Design template ❶

Bench tool kit, page 9

Soldering kit, page 9

Burnisher

FINISHED SIZE
Pendant, 1½ x 1 inch
(3.8 x 2.5 cm)

→ → → Go

1. Arrange the fine silver scrap into seven small piles on a compressed charcoal block. Melt the piles into silver balls of various sizes. Quench each ball in water and set aside.

2. Arrange the balls into a design you like, or use the design template as a guide, making sure to incorporate the bezel.

3. Solder the balls and the bezel together two at a time, then rearrange the soldered pairs into the pendant shape and finish soldering.

4. Solder one closed jump ring to the top of the pendant, parallel with the pendant.

5. Finish the pendant with a brass brush. Use a burnisher to bezel set the 6-mm garnet.

6. Use chain-nose and flat-nose pliers to attach the remaining 4-mm jump ring to the bail and to the ball chain.

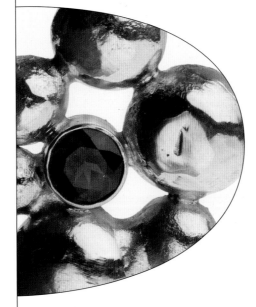

❶
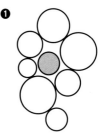

**ROLLER PRINTING • SAWING • FILING • FORMING
SOLDERING • HAMMERING • POLISHING**

➤➤ **Get Set**

5 round copper washers,
  19 gauge, each
  14.3 mm OD

Sterling silver tube,
  4 mm OD

Sterling silver round wire,
  18 gauge, 2⅜ inches
  (6 cm)

Stainless steel neck wire,
  16 or 18 inches
  (40.6 or 45.7 cm)

Bench tool kit, page 9

Soldering kit, page 9

Sandpaper, 100 grit

Planishing hammer

Ring mandrel

Bracelet mandrel

FINISHED SIZE
Pendant, 1¾ x 1¾ inches
(4.4 x 4.4 cm)

➤➤➤ **Go**

1. Use a rolling mill to roller print the texture of the 100-grit sandpaper onto all five copper washers. Once rolled, the washers will be curved. Leave them this way.

2. With a jeweler's saw, cut a 4-mm length of the sterling silver tubing. Lightly file the cut ends. While holding the tube in a pair of flat-nose pliers, file a flat area on one side of the tube. This is the bail for the pendant.

3. Form the 18-gauge sterling silver wire into a circle around a ring mandrel. Solder the ends of the wire circle together. Flatten the wire circle with a planishing hammer.

4. Place the rolled washers upside down on a soldering block and arrange them into a flower design. Solder the silver wire circle to the washers, making sure it does not show on the front.

5. Solder the flat side of the tube bail to the top of a washer, making sure it does not show on the front of the pendant.

6. Using a rawhide mallet, gently hammer the copper ovals on a bracelet mandrel to work harden the metal.

7. Polish the edges of the pendant with fine-grit sandpaper. Slide the neck wire through the silver bail.

Have Time to Spare?

Add a heat patina to the pendant. This one-of-a-kind coloring looks great on copper.

ROLLER PRINTING • SAWING • FILING • SANDING • WIREWORK
SOLDERING • FORGING • ADDING A PATINA • FINISHING

▶ ▶ Get Set

Copper sheet, 22 gauge,
    4 x 3 inches
    (10.2 x 7.6 cm) or to fit
    dried leaf

Scrap wire for scoring leaf
    in rolling mill, 26 gauge,
    8 inches (20.3 cm)

Sterling silver round wire,
    12 gauge, 24 inches
    (61 cm)

Bench tool kit, page 9

Soldering kit, page 9

Dried leaf to use as rolling
    mill texture

Rolling mill

Ball-peen hammer

Bracelet mandrel or
    neck form

Liver of sulfur

Steel wool, extra fine

Brass brush

FINISHED SIZE
Pendant, 5 x 1½ inches
(12.7 x 3.8 cm)

▶ ▶ ▶ Go

1. Position the dried leaf on the copper sheet. Roll these materials through the rolling mill to emboss the metal with the leaf texture. With bench shears or a jeweler's saw, cut out the embossed metal.

2. Place the 26-gauge scrap wire on the centerline of the copper leaf. Roll the leaf and wire through the rolling mill to score the centerline. File and sand the edges of the copper leaf.

3. Cut a ¾-inch (1.9 cm) piece of the sterling silver round wire. Bend the wire into a U shape and file the ends flush.

4. Position the U-shape wire on the back (unscored) side of the copper leaf, near one end and straddling the centerline. Solder the wire onto the leaf with easy solder.

5. Use your fingers to form the remaining silver wire into a large U-shape neck wire. Bend the ends into curvy squiggles as you like. Hammer the curves of the neck wire flat with a ball-peen hammer on a neck form or other curved surface such as a bracelet mandrel. Sand the neck wire.

6. Flatten a ½ inch (1.3 cm) section of one end of the neck wire with a hammer. Position the flattened wire section on the back of the copper leaf, on the centerline and across from the soldered wire. Solder the flat wire section to the copper leaf.

7. Apply a liver-of-sulfur solution only to the copper leaf. Rinse and dry the metal. Buff the leaf with extra fine steel wool to remove excess patina, leaving a dark finish in the recessed areas. Brush the sterling silver neck wire with a brass brush to finish.

➤ Get Ready

**SAWING • STAMPING • DAPPING • FILING • DRILLING
FORGING • POLISHING • BALLING WIRE • WIREWORK**

➤➤ ▶ Get Set

Sterling silver sheet,
18 gauge,
1¼ x 1¼ inches
(3.2 x 3.2 cm)

Smooth stone, ¾ x ½ inch
(1.9 x 1.3 cm)

Sterling silver round wire,
14 gauge, 2 inches
(5.1 cm)

2 sterling silver jump rings,
20 gauge, each 4 mm

Sterling silver curb chain,
3 mm, 18 inches
(45.7 cm)

Bench tool kit, page 9

Soldering kit, page 9

Circle template, 1¼ inches
(3.2 cm) diameter

.925 stamp

Round diamond-tip burr,
3 mm

Gray pumice wheel

Pink rubber polishing
wheel

FINISHED SIZE
Pendant, 1¼ x 1¼ inches
(3.2 x 3.2 cm)

DESIGNER'S NOTE
These instructions are for
making the pendant with a
captured stone (far right),
but as you can see, many
variations are possible.

▶ ▶ ▶ Go

1. Using a circle template and scribe, mark a circle with a 1¼ inch (3.2 cm) diameter on the sterling silver sheet. Cut out the marked circle with a jeweler's saw.

2. Stamp the back of the silver disk with the .925 stamp, 3 mm from the edge. Slightly dome the disk with a hammer and punch in a dapping block.

3. Texture the inside of the silver dome with the round diamond burr in the flexible shaft. File the edge of the domed disk flat.

4. Place your stone in the concave side of the silver dome. With the scribe, mark four points on the dome—two on either side of the stone at the top and two on either side of the stone at the bottom and each 4 to 5 mm from the stone. Drill a hole at each marked point.

5. Cut two lengths of wire, one 1¼ inches (3.2 cm) and the other 1 inch (2.5 cm) long. Place the wires one by one over the stone where they will later hold it in place. Use a scribe to mark the area where the stone touches the wire. Forge the wire between the marks. Polish and slightly curve the wires.

6. Insert the 1-inch (2.5-cm) wire into the bottom two holes, fit the stone underneath the wire, and ball the wire ends on the back of the dome.

7. Insert the 1¼-inch (3.2-cm) wire into the two top holes, and forge the wire ends sticking out the back of the dome flat. Drill a 1-mm hole in each forged wire on the back of the dome.

8. Polish the back of the pendant with a muslin wheel and rouge. Polish the front outside edge of the pendant with a gray pumice wheel followed by a pink rubber wheel.

9. Snip the chain in half, and use the two 4-mm jump rings to attach each end of the chain to each side of the pendant through the holes drilled in step 7.

VARIATION

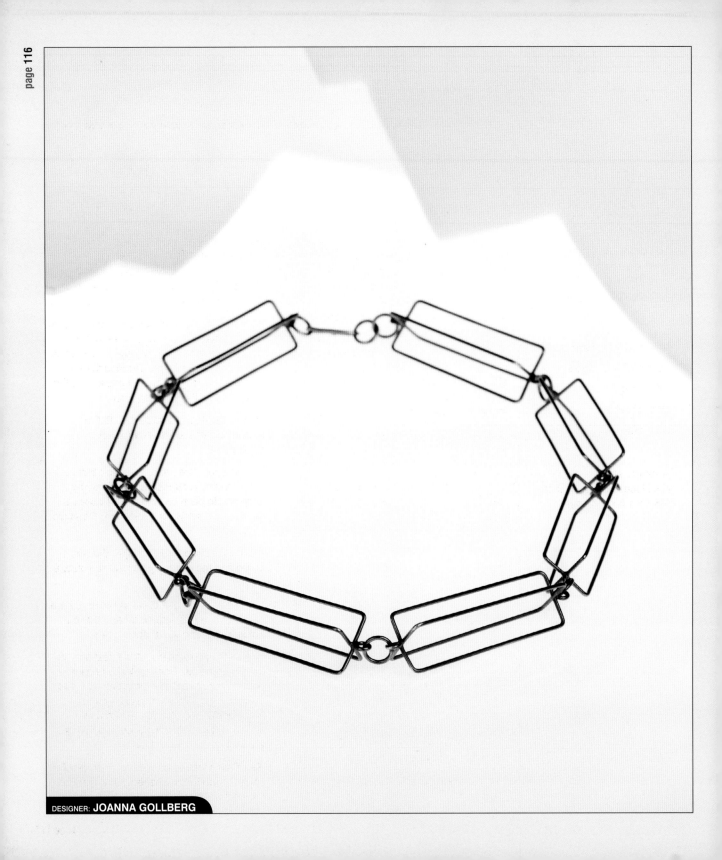

▶▶ ▶ Get Set

Sterling silver round wire, 18 gauge, 7½ feet (2.3 m)

16 sterling silver jump rings, 18 gauge, each 3 mm

10 sterling silver jump rings, 18 gauge, each 6 mm

Bench tool kit, page 9

Soldering kit, page 9

Draw tongs

Liver of sulfur

Steel wool

FINISHED SIZE
Necklace, 18 x ½ x ½ inch (45.7 x 1.3 x 1.3 cm)

▶ ▶ ▶ Go

1. Cut three lengths of the 18-gauge sterling silver wire, each 30 inches (76.2 cm) long. One at a time, straighten each wire by securing one end in a vise and pulling the other end with draw tongs. Use snips to cut eight 5-inch (12.7 cm) wire lengths and sixteen 2½-inch (6.4 cm) wire lengths.

2. Place a 5-inch (12.7 cm) wire on a flat soldering block. Position a 2½-inch (6.4 cm) silver wire piece on both sides of the 5-inch (12.7 cm) wire, centered along its width and forming a cross shape. Solder the joint.

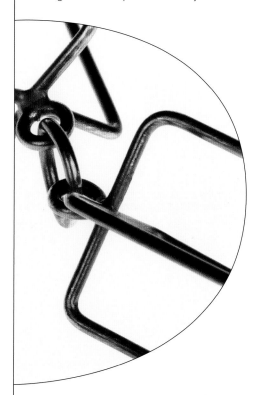

3. Use flat-nose pliers to bend up each segment of the wire cross shape at a 90-degree angle, ¼ inch (6 mm) away from the solder joint. From this bend, mark and snip each wire to measure 2 inches (5.1 cm).

4. Measure and mark ¼ inch (6 mm) in from the unsoldered end of each wire. With flat-nose pliers, make a 90-degree bend in each wire at the marked point. Arrange the ends of the wires with your fingers or pliers so they touch. Solder the ends together.

5. Repeat steps 2 through 4 with the remaining wires to create a total of eight boxes.

6. Use chain-nose and flat-nose pliers to close the smaller jump rings. Solder one jump ring to each end of the wire boxes at the previous solder joint, bisecting the angle of the wires.

7. Use flat-nose pliers to adjust the wire boxes and the jump rings so they are straight and even.

8. Using round-nose pliers, make an S hook with the 18-gauge wire, and ball the ends. Solder one end of the S hook closed.

9. Attach each wire box to the next one with 6-mm jump rings. Connect the S-hook to one end with one 6-mm jump ring. Connect the remaining two 6-mm jump rings to the opposite end. Solder all jump rings closed and sand the necklace with 400-grit sandpaper.

10. Patina the necklace with a liver-of-sulfur solution. Rub the blackened metal with fine-grit steel wool.

▶▶ ▶ Get Set

44 sterling silver oval
   stampings,
   each 6 x 12 mm

Sterling silver wire,
   16 gauge, ½ inch
   (1.3 cm)

Fine silver wire, 22 gauge,
   24 inches (61 cm)

Bench tool kit, page 9

Soldering kit, page 9

Tumbler

FINISHED SIZE
Chain, 16½ inches
(42 cm) long

DESIGNER'S NOTE
This necklace can also
be made from many
other hand-sawn or
precut shapes.

▶ ▶ ▶ Go

1. With a center punch, mark and drill two 0.75-mm holes in each silver oval piece, centered and approximately 2 to 3 mm from each edge.

2. On one silver oval, enlarge one of the drilled holes with a 1.5-mm bit. Saw a slit 1.5-mm wide to the center of the piece, making a "keyhole." On another silver oval, enlarge an existing hole to 1.3 mm. These ovals will be the clasp (see photo below).

3. Fit the length of 16-gauge sterling silver wire through the 1.3-mm hole drilled in step 2 and solder. Using snips, trim the wire to 6 mm. Ball the end of the wire with a torch. File the other end of the wire flush with the surface of the oval. This is the "key." Make sure the key fits into the keyhole sawed in step 2. If not, re-drill the hole with a larger bit at the end of the slit in the center of the oval.

4. Cut 43 pieces of the 22-gauge fine silver wire, each ½ inch (1.3 cm) long. Ball one end of each wire length with a torch. Thread a balled, fine silver wire through the holes of the 20 silver ovals. Trim each wire to 2 to 3 mm long.

5. Lay the silver ovals on a soldering brick with the un-balled ends sticking up, and thread each wire though another silver oval, creating a chain. Ball the ends of each wire that sticks up. Make sure to position the ovals with the key and the keyhole at opposite ends of the chain.

6. Pickle the necklace, and then polish it in a tumbler with stainless steel shot.

→ Get Ready

►► Get Set

Sterling silver sheet,
28 gauge, 1 ¾ x ⅞ inch
(4.4 x 2.2 cm)

Gold-filled square wire,
14 karat, 16 gauge,
5 inches (12.7 cm)

Gold-filled bezel strip,
30 gauge, 2 mm wide,
¾ inch (1.9 cm)

Peach moonstone,
8 x 10 mm

Sterling silver sheet, 26
gauge, 10 x 12 mm

Sterling silver tubing,
4.5 mm OD, ½ inch
(1.3 cm)

Sterling silver sheet,
18 gauge, 3 x 3 mm

Sterling silver tubing, 3.5
mm OD, ¾ inch (1.9 cm)

2 round faceted amethysts,
2 to 3 mm, optional

Bench tool kit, page 9

Soldering kit, page 9

Liver of sulfur

Epoxy

Black satin cord, 3 mm,
30 inches (76.2 cm)

Industrial tube ringer

Miter jig

Small chisel

FINISHED SIZE
Pendant, 1½ x ⅞ inch
(3.8 x 2.2 cm)

►►► Go

1. Anneal the 26-gauge sterling silver sheet. Run the annealed sheet through a tube ringer in one direction, anneal the metal, and then run it back through the tube ringer in the opposite direction. Note: The second pass is much harder than the first. You'll need to use a bench vise to hold the wringer and use large pliers for leverage while turning the knob.

2. Create a 2-mm-wide flat strip on each edge of the textured sheet by hammering the edges with a hammer and a flat punch.

3. Cut four pieces of 16-gauge square gold-filled wire: two 40 mm long and two 20 mm long. Use a miter jig to file 45° angles on each wire end. Arrange the wires into a frame and solder together with gold-filled solder. Solder the gold-wire frame to the corrugated 26-gauge silver sheet. Use a hammer and small chisel to texture the frame.

4. Use the 30-gauge gold-filled bezel strip to make a bezel for the moonstone. Solder the bezel to a piece of 26-gauge sterling silver

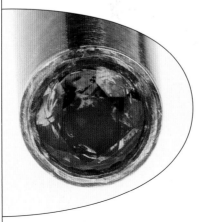

sheet. Trim, file, and sand the bezel cup. Position the bezel cup on the corrugated silver sheet, centered and 8 mm from the bottom edge. Sweat solder the setting to the sheet.

5. To make the bail, anneal the 4.5-mm silver tubing and curve it slightly with your fingers. Cut a 9.5-mm length of the tubing. Solder the tubing to the 3-mm-square, 18-gauge sterling silver sheet. File the top ends of the tube bail at a slight angle. Sand the bail and solder it to the top center of the pendant.

6. To make a slide so the cord is adjustable, cut a 5-mm piece of the 4.5-mm sterling silver tubing. Use a center punch and hammer to flare both ends of the tube. To make end caps for the cord, cut two pieces of the 3.5-mm tubing, each 8mm long. Optional: Tube set a 3-mm amethyst in one end of each end cap using the flex shaft.

7. Use a liver-of-sulfur solution to add a patina the metal pieces. Polish the pieces with a brass brush. Use a burnisher to set the moonstone into the bezel.

8. Thread a 30-inch (76.2-cm) length of 3-mm satin cord through the bail. Thread both ends of the cord through the adjustment slide. Adhere the end caps to the cord with epoxy.

DESIGNER'S NOTE
Tube setting amethysts into the end caps is a lovely finishing touch but adds an extra degree of difficulty (and a few more minutes!) to this project. If you've got the skills and the time, however, definitely go for this option.

DESIGNER: **SARA WESTERMARK**

→ Get Ready

SAWING • FILING • SANDING • ROLLER PRINTING • USING A DISK CUTTER
DRILLING • SOLDERING • BALLING WIRE • RIVETING • ADDING A PATINA

►► Get Set

Copper sheet, 18 gauge,
  4 x 2½ inches
  (10.2 x 6.4 cm)

Sterling silver sheet,
  22 gauge, 3½ x 2 inches
  (8.9 x 5.1 cm)

2 sterling silver jump rings,
  18 gauge, each 8 mm

Sterling silver round wire,
  18 gauge, 12 inches,
  (30.5 cm)

Stainless steel neck cord
  with clasp, 16 inches
  (40.6 cm)

Photocopied design
  templates ❶ and ❷,
  enlarged 200%

Bench tool kit, page 9

Soldering kit, page 9

Wrinkled tissue paper or
  paper towel

Rolling mill

Disk cutter

Liver of sulfur

Steel wool, extra fine

FINISHED SIZE
Pendant, 1¾ x 3¾ inches
(4.4 x 9.5 cm)

DESIGNER'S NOTE
Instead of using a rolling
mill, you can texture the
metal with different ham-
mers, through reticulation,
or by purchasing patterned
sterling silver sheet.

►►► Go

1. Using the photocopied design templates, transfer the large moon shape onto the copper sheet and the small moon shape onto the silver sheet. Use a jeweler's saw to cut out the moon shapes, and file and sand their edges.

2. Fold the crinkled tissue paper in half and place the silver moon inside the paper. Roll this stack through the rolling mill to transfer the texture of the paper onto the metal.

3. Use disk cutters to cut out circles on the silver moon in a random pattern. Cut partial circles on the edge of the silver moon. Vary the sizes of the circles with the largest being 1 inch (2.5 cm) in diameter.

4. Using the project photo as a guide, use a center punch to mark the holes for the rivets on the silver moon. Drill each hole with a 1.2-mm bit. Sand the drilled holes to remove any burrs.

5. Center the silver moon on top of the copper moon. Using the holes drilled in the silver moon as a guide, drill the holes in the copper. Sand the holes to remove any burrs.

6. Mark the two holes at the top points of the copper form, and drill with a 1.2-mm bit. Attach a jump ring through each hole, and solder closed.

7. Use snips to cut 13 rivets from the 18-gauge round silver wire, each ¾ inch (1.9 cm) long. Ball one end of each rivet wire with a torch. Pickle the balled rivet wires.

8. From the front side of the pendant, thread one balled rivet wire through a matching hole in the silver and copper moons. Trim the wire so that 1 mm extends past the back of the pendant. Rivet the wire, flattening the balled head in the process. Repeat this step for all remaining rivets.

9. Patina the pendant with a liver-of-sulfur solution. Rinse and dry the piece. Buff the pendant with extra fine steel wool to remove excess patina, leaving a dark finish in the recesses. Thread the steel cable through the two jump rings on the pendant.

❶
❷

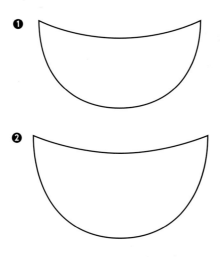

→ Get Ready

**PIERCING • SAWING • FILING • SANDING
DIE FORMING • KUM BOO • SOLDERING • POLISHING**

▶ ▶ Get Set

Steel or brass sheet,
20 gauge, 1½ x 1½
inches (3.8 x 3.8 cm)

Gold leaf, 24 karat,
40 x 40 x 0.1 mm

Copper sheet, 18 gauge,
5 x 5 inches
(12.7 x 12.7 cm)

Fine silver sheet, 18 gauge,
40 x 40 x 1 mm

Oval jump ring, 20 gauge,
6 x 8 mm

Photocopied design
template ❶

Bench tool kit, page 9

Soldering kit, page 9

Urethane pad, ⅛ inch
(3 mm) thick,
80 hardness

Hydraulic press

Electric hotplate

Burnishers

Bowl of ice water

FINISHED SIZE
Pendant, 1¼ x 1¼ inches
(3.2 x 3.2 cm)

▶ ▶ ▶ Go

1. Adhere the photocopied design template to the steel or brass sheet. Pierce and saw out the design. File and sand all cut edges smooth. This will be the die.

2. Place the gold leaf under the die and on top of the urethane pad. Insert the stack in the center of the hydraulic press and apply a pressure of 250 bar or 3625 psi.

3. Separate the gold leaf from the die. If some sections of the pattern remain stuck to the gold leaf, delicately detach them with tweezers.

4. Place the copper sheet on the hotplate and adjust to highest temperature. Put the gold leaf design in the center of the silver sheet and place on the copper sheet. Let the silver and gold heat for five minutes while the burnishers cool in the ice water.

5. Dry the burnishers. Use one to keep the gold foil and silver sheet in position on the hotplate. Use the other burnisher to make small movements with gentle pressure on the gold foil, pressing the foil onto the silver sheet. When your burnisher starts to adhere to the metal, cool it in the water and dry it again. Repeat the process until the gold is well adhered to the silver. Cool the silver in the bowl of water.

6. Place the silver sheet on the urethane pad, with the die carefully positioned on top of the gold leaf. Insert the stack in the center of the hydraulic press, and apply a pressure of 300 bar or 4351 psi. Check the results, and repeat using more pressure if necessary.

7. Gently throw the piece on a wooden floor to separate the silver from the die.

8. Use a saw to cut out the center of the piece and its outline. Drill a 1-mm hole, near the top edge, between two silver bumps. Sand all edges smooth.

9. Thread the oval jump ring through the drill hole and solder it closed. Polish the edges and both faces.

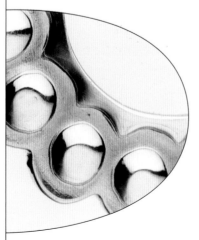

❶

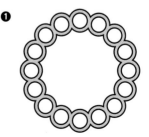

DESIGNER: **JUAN CARLOS CABALLERO-PEREZ**

SAWING • ANNEALING • DAPPING • MELTING METAL • ROLLER PRINTING
HAMMERING • FORMING • SOLDERING • FILING • FINISHING
BEZEL SETTING

▶▶ Get Set

Sterling silver tubing, 5 mm OD, 2 inches (5.1 cm)

Yellow gold wire, 22 karat, 24 gauge, 3 inches, (7.6 cm)

Bimetal sheet, 18 karat gold and sterling silver, 22 gauge, 1⅛ x 2⅞ inches (2.9 x 7.3 cm)

Sterling silver sheet, 22 gauge, 1⅛ x 2⅞ inches (2.9 x 7.3 cm)

Sterling silver wire, 12 gauge, 2 inches (5.1 cm)

Onyx cabochon, 4.5 mm

Bench tool kit, page 9

Soldering kit, page 9

Heavyweight paper

Craft knife

Rolling mill

Cross-peen hammer

Bracelet mandrel

Brass brush

Bezel pusher

FINISHED SIZE
Pendant, 2¾ x 1⅛ x ⁵⁄₁₆ inch (7 x 2.9 x 0.8 cm)

DESIGNER'S NOTE
If you don't own a bracelet mandrel, almost any cylindrical object, such as a baseball bat or a large round pipe, will work.

▶▶▶ Go

1. Cut two pieces of the 5-mm tubing with a jeweler's saw: one 9 mm (for the bail) and one 3 mm (for the bezel). Anneal the 9-mm tube and both pieces of sheet metal. Flare both ends of the 9-mm tube with a 7-mm dapping punch.

2. Cut the 22-karat gold wire into six ½-inch (1.3 cm) lengths. Use a torch to melt the wires into six granules on a charcoal block.

3. From a 1¼ x 3-inch (3.2 x 7.6 cm) piece of heavyweight paper, use a craft knife to cut out a series of twelve horizontal rectangular shapes, arranged randomly. Carefully position the paper on the bimetal sheet, and roll this stack through the rolling mill.

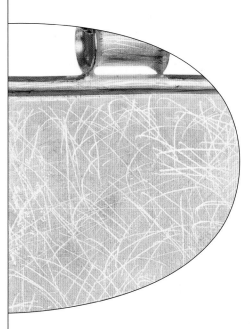

Measure the bimetal sheet and the sterling silver sheet metal to make sure they are still the same size. If not, trim any excess metal with a saw.

4. Measure and mark a trapezoid on the bottom of the bimetal sheet that measures 8 mm on one side and 13 mm on the other side (the width of the metal sheet). Saw out the marked shape.

5. With a cross-peen hammer, texture each side edge of the bimetal sheet and the sterling silver sheet. Bend each metal piece over a bracelet mandrel so they are slightly curved.

6. Position the bimetal sheet on top of the silver sheet with the curves facing opposite directions. Line up the top edges of the metal and solder them together. File the soldered seam, then solder the 2-inch (5.1 cm) piece of 12-gauge wire to the seam. Do NOT pickle. File off the excess wire so the ends are flush.

7. Center and solder the tube bail on top of the round wire. Solder the gold granules onto the bimetal sheet. Solder the 5-mm tube into place for the stone setting. Once all soldering is completed, pickle and rinse the pendant.

8. Coat the entire pendant in flux, heat it until the flux is clear, and then pickle the pendant again. Rinse and brass-brush the bimetal.

9. Set the stone in the tube setting with a bezel pusher. Burnish all edges of the pendant, including the edges of the bail. Scratch the front and back of the sterling silver sheet to give it texture.

▶▶ **Get Set**

Sterling silver medium-wall
   tubing, 3 mm OD,
   5½ inches (14 cm)

Yellow gold saucer beads,
   14 karat, 3.5 mm

Yellow gold round wire,
   14 karat, 22 gauge

Sterling silver tubing,
   4 mm OD, 5 mm

Sterling silver snake chain
   with clasp, 2 mm,
   16 inches (40.6 cm)

Bench tool kit, page 9

Soldering kit, page 9

Hart burr, 3 mm

Cup burr, 3.2 mm

Liver of sulfur

Brass brush

FINISHED SIZE
Pendant, 2 x ¼ x ¼ inch
(5.1 x 6 x 6 cm)

▶▶▶ **Go**

1. Using a hart burr in a flexible shaft, texture the 3-mm, medium-wall sterling silver tubing. With a jeweler's saw, cut 11 segments of the textured tubing, each 12.5 mm. De-burr the cut ends with a cup burr.

2. Secure a center punch in a vise. Flare the ends of each piece of tubing simultaneously by placing one end on the center punch in the vise and using another center punch and hammer to flare the opposite end.

3. With the corner of a flat file, make V-shaped grooves in a charcoal block to keep the tubing segments aligned for soldering. With a gold saucer bead between each segment, solder together two sets of four tubing segments and one set of three tubing segments. (These are the sticks of "bamboo.")

4. Cut a 6-inch (15.2 cm) length of 22-gauge, 14-karat gold round wire and anneal it dead soft. Arrange the three sticks of bamboo so two pieces are next to each other and one piece rests on top. Wrap the wire around the middle of the pieces and solder the ends.

5. Solder the 5-mm length of 4-mm silver tubing horizontally to the back of the pendant, 10 mm from the top edge.

6. Patina the piece with a liver-of-sulfur solution. Polish it with a brass brush.

CONTRIBUTING DESIGNERS

2 Roses Studio, located in Southern California, is an artistic collaboration between metalsmith Corliss Rose and lapidary artist John Lemieux Rose. Each is a master craftsman with a distinctive style and unique artistic vision. The studio is driven by the principles of exploration and experimentation through the use of unorthodox materials and techniques. E-mail tworoses@2roses.com or visit www.2roses.com.

Erica Stankwytch Bailey works from her studio in Fayetteville, North Carolina. She remarks, "I have my head about 10 inches from a piece of jewelry most of the time." Erica is a full-time metalsmith and workshop instructor. Find her at www.ericastankwytchbailey.com.

Jacqueline Barbera studied jewelry and metalsmithing at the University of Oregon. Her work comments on ideas of beauty, status, and adornment. See her website at www.jbarbera.com.

Monika Becker is an honors graduate from the Ontario College of Art and Design in Toronto, Ontario, where she studied jewelry and metalsmithing. She currently runs a jewelry business from her studio in Cobourg, Ontario. For more information and to view her latest collections, visit www.lifeforms-art.com.

Juan Carlos Caballero-Perez is a metal artist and educator who came to the United States in 1986 from Mexico City, Mexico. Carlos works as an associate professor in the metals program at Rochester Institute of Technology, where he started in 2001, following receipt of bachelor's and master's degrees from the same institute. A New York State Foundation of the Arts Fellow and Craft Alliance of New York State Career Development Grant recipient, Carlos creates jewelry and large public sculptures out of his Rochester, New York, studio.

Charles Carubia started making jewelry in the 1970s while studying at the School of Visual Arts in New York. He is a member of the Florida Society of Goldsmiths and the Saint Augustine Art Association. Charles specializes in custom design and makes one-of-a-kind pieces that incorporate 30 years of knowledge. Contact him at carubias@bellsouth.net.

Sunyoung Cheong is a metalsmith and jewelry designer living in Kansas. Her work is focused on body adornment, primarily using techniques such as fabrication, casting, enameling, and CAD. She often incorporates textiles and fiber techniques into her jewelry designs.

Mimi Cheung uses traditional metalsmithing techniques to create jewelry, primarily from sterling silver. Her work is inspired by the sculptural facets of architecture, the perfection in nature, the wonder of travel, and the tradition of tribal and ethnic arts. She continues to study and explore this craft, and her current creations can be found at www.alittleluster.com.

Linda Chow is an award-winning goldsmith and jewelry artist. She has been creating both traditional jewelry and wearable sculpture for over twenty years, with work exhibited and collected nationally and internationally. As an educator and an active metal artist, she continues to explore with unusual sculptural forms, nonprecious metals, and recycled materials.

Vicki Cook lives and hammers in southwest Michigan, where she is a proud member of Chartreuse Co-op Art Gallery. She teaches small-scale metalworking techniques at Krasl Art Center in St. Joseph, Michigan, and at the Kalamazoo Institute of Art in Kalamazoo, Michigan. Her website is www.vcmetalworks.com, and her adventures in hammering are at www.vicki-cook.blogspot.com.

Louisa Crispin grew up in a small village in England with views of the North Downs. Leisure time was spent in the woods, orchards, and hop fields, where she came to love nature. She is particularly affected by shadows and textures, which often inspire her work. Louisa produces limited edition pieces in sterling silver, highlighted with semi precious stones. In her early thirties, she took classes in silversmithing, and thanks to a stimulating teacher, a tolerant family, and supportive friends, she now has a successful small business doing what she loves.

Tina Lee Degreef is inspired by nature and her culture. She enjoys creating jewelry that is organic, presenting it in its simplest forms.

Nina Dinoff creates jewelry that focuses on the interplay of simple geometric form with the complex, organic nature of the body. Her work is influenced by her background in graphic design and by her love of modernism. She lives and works in Brooklyn, New York. You can see her work at www.ninadinoffjewelry.com.

Aimee Domash is a bench jeweler who works mostly with sterling silver; however, she adds color to her designs with gold, enamel, gemstones, and resin. She particularly enjoys making elegant and clean-lined jewelry, as well as sculptural pieces. To view more of Aimee's work, visit www.salmonrockstudio.com.

Thomasin Durgin is a Memphis-based artist who received an MFA from the Memphis College of Art in 2001. Her mixed-metal jewelry can be seen at www.thomasin.com and at www.etsy.com under the name MetalRiot.

Dilyana Evtimova lives and works in West Midlands, United Kingdom. She graduated in 2007 from the University of Wolverhampton in three-dimensional contemporary applied arts. She was then selected as a jeweler in residence at Bilston Craft Gallery, designing and making jewelry for retail and private commissions. She strives to capture the beauty and fragility of organic forms in her work. Email: dilyanadesigns@hotmail.co.uk.

Sarah Gazie is a jewelry designer based in Perth, Australia. Using materials including polymer clay, resin, and vintage items, Sarah creates jewelry under the label Odd Girl Outz: www.oddgirlout.com.au.

Elizabeth Glass Geltman and Rachel Geltman are a mother-and-daughter jewelry design team in Washington, D.C. Their creations have been published in numerous books, magazines, and newspapers. Visit them at www.geltdesigns.com.

Joanna Gollberg is a studio jeweler in Asheville, North Carolina. In addition to making jewelry, she is the author of four Lark Craft books: *Making Metal Jewelry*, *Creative Metal Crafts*, *The Art and Craft of Making Jewelry*, and *The Ultimate Jeweler's Guide*. Joanna teaches jewelry making at craft schools, such as The Penland School of Craft and Arrowmont Craft School, as well as for metalsmithing groups across the country. She exhibits her work nationally at fine craft shows and galleries.

Kim Harrell lived, worked, and studied in London, England, from 1989 to 2003. She returned home to Colorado in 2003 and established her design studio (www.kimharrell.blogspot.com) and a high-end craft gallery, East End Applied Arts (www.eastendarts.com). Inspired by her "less is more" design philosophy, Kim is always expanding and developing new collections for wholesale, retail, and private clients.

Catherine Hodge is a jewelry designer, former teacher, and current stay-at-home mom to two little boys. She creates jewelry with a focus on texture, feminine elements, and little touches of whimsy. See more of her work at www.catherinemarissa.com or contact her at www.catherinemarissa.etsy.com.

Peter Hoogeboom is a designer from Amsterdam, Netherlands. He believes that the worktable of a contemporary jeweler is both the perfect travel-ground for someone who likes adventure, in any shape and any material, and a great platform for one who also wants to stay in control. Visit www.peterhoogeboom.nl.

Steven James is always armed with his mantra, "What are you gonna make today?" He is a lifelong craft dabbler who incorporates creativity into everyday living. Join him in the fun by visiting his website, www.macaroniandglitter.com, or follow him at www.facebook.com/stevenjames.

Seongbun Kim is an enamellist, jeweler, and metalsmith. She studied jewelry design at Pratt Institute in New York and tries to apply her energy to all areas of jewelry. She finds inspiration in every single moment, and can even be motivated by a blunt neighbor. Recently one of her enamel rings was selected and published in Lark Craft's *500 Enameled Objects*.

Taya and Silvija Koschnick grew up working in their mother's bead store (www.beadparadise.com) where they came to appreciate designing with rare and unusual beads. They formed Tasi Designs jewelry

in Portland, Oregon (www.tasidesigns.com). Tasi Designs blends new, antique, and ancient components to create unique jewelry with a modern aesthetic.

Isabelle Lamontagne graduated from a Quebec, Canada, Cégep jewelry program in 2008. She strives to create jewels that can be modified and worn in more than one way. Contact her at isa.lamontagne@hotmail.com.

Ann L. Lumsden is a goldsmith, designer, and Ottawa, Canada native. She strives to create pieces that are contemporary and classic. Through ongoing explorations of materials and techniques, both traditional and avant-garde, her work continues to evolve. She is a member of the Metal Arts Guild of Canada, and her pieces have twice been named Best in Show in their annual juried exhibitions.

Susan Machamer is a professional metalsmith, designer, and gemologist who co-owns Cazenovia Jewelry, Inc., in Upstate New York. She enjoys designing one-of-a-kind pieces, using fine metals and unusual gemstones. Her work has a strong connection to natural forms and textures. See www.cazjewelry.com.

Rebeca Mojica is an award-winning chainmaille artist and instructor. She knows more than 100 weaves and is the founder of Blue Buddha Boutique, one of the largest chainmaille suppliers in the world. See her creations at www.BlueBuddhaBoutique.com.

Nathalie Mornu recently discovered leather as a material, and she's filled with regret for the years she could have spent building a hoard of skins and creating magic with them. Nathalie works as an editor at Lark Crafts. She's dabbled in many crafts, and periodically creates projects for Lark publications—beaded jewelry, a re-upholstered mid-century chair, a weird scarecrow made from cutlery, and a gingerbread igloo. She authored *Leather Jewelry* (2010), *Quilt It with Wool* (2009), and *A Is for Apron* (2008), and she's now working on a book of projects made from repurposed scarves.

Stephanie Morton lives and works in Toronto, Ontario. The pebble used in her necklace was picked up in an area of Toronto known as "the beach," where she takes her large, goofy dog to swim. Her work can be found at www.madpashdesigns.com.

Rachel Alexander Quinn is a jewelry designer who feels that working in the art of adornment is a stimulating marriage of creativity and function. She finds inspiration in strong form and the spaces it encapsulates, examples of which can be found on her website: www.rachelalexanderquinn.com. Rachel lives and works in New York City with her dog Max.

Tiina Rajakallio is a Finnish jewellery artist and designer living and working in Lappeenranta, Finland. She studied jewelry art and stone product design in both Finland and Sweden.

Karine Rodrigue lives in Quebec City, Canada, and has been a jeweler for six years. She specializes in improbable technical and aesthetic experimentations. In the future, she would like to devote herself to researching contemporary jewelry. Visit www.naphtalenefabrik.blogspot.com.

Davina Romansky is a metals artist incorporating the use of natural tension and movements found in nature. She gives artistic identity to each work by combining conceptual and aesthetic beauty with technical proficiency. Davina has a BFA in metals from Rochester Institute of Technology and holds numerous design awards. Website: www.davinaromansky.com.

Ada Rosman's work is continually influenced by her love of traveling, seeing new places, encountering new cultures, and meeting new people. Her inspiration ranges from patterns, textiles, and textures, to architecture and anything that brings back memories. Travel with her at www.adarosman.com.

John A. Sartin is an award-winning jewelry artist who merges new and old fabrication techniques to create truly original pieces of wearable art. The driving influence behind his work is the challenge to conceptualize a piece, then to solve all the problems that arise in the making of that piece. Currently residing in Albuquerque, New Mexico, his work can be seen at art fairs and festivals or on his website www.johnsartindesigns.com.

Brenda Schweder is the author of *Junk to Jewelry* and *Vintage Redux*. A frequent BeadStyle contributor, Brenda has been published in all of Kalmbach Publishing's jewelry titles, as well as a number of pamphlets. Her newest book of fabulous projects is called *Steel Wire Jewelry* (Lark Crafts, 2010). Brenda is a Crystallized Swarovski Elements Ambassador. E-mail at b@brendaschweder.com, or visit her at www.brendaschweder.com or www.brendaschwederjewelry/blogspot.com.

Danielle Lauren Smith graduated with a BFA in jewelry and metals from the Cleveland Institute of Art. Recently, she has been working with bird breeders, creating feather jewelry. This pursuit is a part of her ongoing research on beauty.

Theresa St. Romain is a metal and jewelry artist living in Atlanta, Georgia. She teaches jewelry and metalsmithing at The Spruill Center for the Arts in Atlanta, Georgia, and at Pratt Fine Arts Center in Seattle, Washington. Her work can be seen at Topaz Gallery in Atlanta, and on her websites:
www.saintromain.com and
www.fireballcollective.com.

Erin Strother is a full-time graphic designer living happily in Southern California with her very supportive husband, George, and her disobedient dog, Swiffer. She loves working with a wide variety of materials and experimenting with unique design styles. Visit www.studioegraphics.com to see more of her work.

Amy Tavern graduated from the University of Washington with a BFA in metal design in 2002. She has taught beginning jewelry classes, has lectured on professional practices, and sells her jewelry in shops and galleries around the United States and at www.amytavern.com.

Victoria Tillotson is a jewelry designer and instructor of jewelry making at the School of Visual Arts in New York City. She is also the author of *Chic Metal: Modern Metal Jewelry to Make at Home*. Victoria's jewelry has been featured in numerous magazines such as *Lucky*, *Allure*, *Essence*, and others. She lives and works in New York City.

John Tzelepis received his undergraduate degree from Skidmore College and his MFA in metals from Arizona State University. He has made jewelry and sculpture for over a decade. He exhibits work nationally and has been featured in several publications. See his work at www.johntzelepis.com.

Ingeborg Vandamme is a jewelry designer living and working in Amsterdam, Netherlands. She experiments with different kinds of materials, such as combinations of paper, textiles, and metal. Her jewelry is featured in numerous Lark Crafts publications, including *The Art of Jewelry: Paper Jewelry*, *The Art of Jewelry: Wood*, *500 Earrings*, *500 Wedding Rings*, *500 Pedants and Lockets*, *500 Enameled Objects*, *Stitched Jewels*, and *30-Minute Earrings*. Website: www.ingeborgvandamme.nl.

Sara Westermark is a self-taught metalsmith who lives in Wilmington, North Carolina. In addition to making jewelry, Sara also teaches classical voice lessons and performs regionally. Sara finds inspiration in nature, chaos, and life lessons while continuing to learn new techniques in the process of metalsmithing.

Marina Zachou works as a jewelry designer and maker. She has taken part in many group exhibitions and fairs and has been awarded numerous times for her designs. Marina works with individual clients, jewelry shops, and at the Museum of Contemporary Art in Athens, Greece.

ABOUT THE AUTHOR

Marthe Le Van is a jewelry editor for Lark Crafts. Since 2000, she has written, edited, juried, or curated more than 40 titles. The books she's authored on making jewelry include *30-Minute Earrings*, *Stitched Jewels*, *Prefab Jewelry*, *Fabulous Jewelry from Found Objects*, and *The Art of Jewelry: Paper Jewelry*. Marthe has also served as the editor for all jewelry books in Lark's popular "500" series, as well as the juror for *500 Wedding Rings* and the curator for *Masters: Gold*. Marthe is a member of the Art Jewelry Forum, The Society of North American Goldsmiths, and the Precious Metal Clay Guild.

ACKNOWLEDGMENTS

After the amazing amount of proposals that came in for the first book in this series, *30-Minute Earrings*, I was anxious to see the response to our designer call-out for *30-Minute Necklaces*. As I had hoped, it was outstanding. I can't thank all the talented designers enough for contributing their ideas and precious time—designers whose work is in these pages and those whose projects we were unable to include. Your dedication never wavers, and your extraordinary effort does not go unnoticed.

I also value the expertise and commitment of the Lark Crafts team that worked on this publication. Art director and cover designer Ginger Graziano did a stellar job with the layout and design, and I'm proud to have collaborated with her on this project. Thanks to Stewart O'Shields for his sparkling and clear photography and Dana Irwin for her distinctive jewelry styling. With enviable efficiency and grace, Gavin Young provided much-appreciated editorial support. I'm grateful for her help every day. Thanks also to Joanna Gollberg for her technical support and editorial eye.

Finally, I'd like to thank our readers for the enthusiasm and passion they have for our books. I hope these designs bring you hours of joy (but only in 30-minute increments). We do it for you!

DESIGNER INDEX

SARAH GAZIA

NINA DINOFF

NATHALIE MORNU

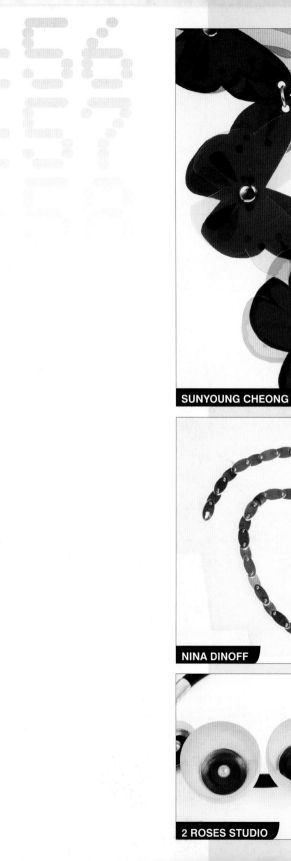

SUNYOUNG CHEONG

NINA DINOFF

2 ROSES STUDIO